Introduction

Overview of Affiliate Marketing

Hello there! Welcome aboard the exciting journey of affiliate marketing. We're thrilled to have you here, and we promise it's going to be an enlightening ride. But before we start exploring the uncharted territories, let's start with a basic orientation.

So, what is affiliate marketing? Think of it as a digital version of a referral program. In the traditional brick-and-mortar world, you'd recommend a product or service to a friend, and if they purchased based on your recommendation, you might get a thank-you or a reward. Affiliate marketing is the online version of that, but on a much larger and more profitable scale.

In the digital space, you − the affiliate − promote a product or service provided by a merchant. This promotion could be through a blog post, a review, a video, or a social media post. In this promotion, you'd provide a unique link or code that leads back to the merchant's site. If someone clicks on this link and makes a purchase, you earn a commission. In other words, you're rewarded for bringing business to the merchant.

And the beauty of it all? You don't have to worry about creating the product, managing the inventory, shipping, customer service, or any of the typical responsibilities of a product owner. Your job is purely promotional. You're the connecting link between the customer and the merchant – and you get paid for it!

The Potential of Affiliate Marketing

You might still be wondering about the potential of affiliate marketing. Is it really as promising as it seems? Could it genuinely transform your financial future? To put your mind at ease and inject a dose of optimism, let's explore in detail the potential of this exciting field.

When we speak of the internet as a marketplace, the scope is literally mind-boggling. Roughly 4.9 billion people across the globe use the internet. Imagine having even a fraction of that audience interested in the products or services you're promoting. Your earning potential skyrockets when your market isn't confined to a physical store or local area. We're playing in a global field here, and that is one of the most enticing aspects of affiliate marketing.

Moreover, consider the variety of products and services available for promotion. Virtually every industry has room for affiliate marketers, whether it's fashion, tech, health and wellness, travel, finance, and many others. You can find a niche that aligns with your passion and interests, making your affiliate marketing journey not only profitable but also enjoyable.

Now let's talk numbers, keeping in mind that earnings can greatly vary. Many affiliate marketers make a few hundred to a few thousand dollars per month, particularly when starting. As they hone their strategies and grow their audience, these numbers can escalate. Top affiliates are known to rake in six or even seven figures annually. It's not a get-rich-quick scheme, but with consistent effort and smart strategies, the financial reward can be substantial.

However, let's also address the elephant in the room. There will be challenges and setbacks. There might be times when you question your decision to dive into affiliate marketing. That's perfectly normal. The path to any worthwhile goal is rarely smooth and straight. But remember, every challenge is an opportunity to learn and grow. And with this guide by your side, you'll have all the tools and knowledge you need to navigate through these obstacles.

The Power of Passive Income

Passive income has long been the holy grail of financial freedom, and for good reason. Imagine earning money while you sleep, while you're on holiday, or while you're busy doing other things. That's the beauty of passive income, and it's at the core of affiliate marketing.

But let's clarify what passive income really means, as it's often misunderstood. Passive doesn't mean no effort is required. Rather, it means the effort is front-loaded. You work hard in the beginning to set up your income stream, and then it continues to generate income with little ongoing effort.

In affiliate marketing, you invest time and energy in the beginning to set up your website or blog, select and join affiliate programs, and create valuable content. But once you've set up these elements, your affiliate links can continue to generate income, even when you're not actively working on your site. Each click on your affiliate link by a potential customer is a potential commission for you. Whether you're asleep or awake, your links are available to your audience around the clock.

However, passive income doesn't mean you can completely neglect your affiliate marketing business after setting it up. Trends change, products evolve, and your audience's interests can shift over time. Regular maintenance and updates will be necessary to keep your business relevant and profitable. But compared to a regular 9-5 job, the time and location flexibility offered by affiliate marketing is incomparable.

The real power of passive income lies in its potential to grant you financial freedom and flexibility. It gives you the opportunity to make money on your own terms, to create a lifestyle that isn't dictated by a traditional job. It's the power to take control of your time and your life. And that, dear reader, is what we aim to help you achieve with this guide.

Who This Book Is For

If you're sitting there right now thinking, "Is this book really for me? Can I do this?" we want you to know something – this book is for you. Yes, you! This guide is for everyone and anyone who has a desire to dive into the world of affiliate marketing.

Are you a complete newbie to this field, having just discovered what affiliate marketing means? Great, you're in the right place. This book will introduce you to the ins and outs of this exciting venture, from the very basics right through to the more complex elements of running your own affiliate marketing business.

Maybe you're a blogger or social media influencer looking to monetize your platform. Fantastic! Affiliate marketing can be an excellent way to earn revenue from your existing audience, and this guide will show you exactly how to do it.

Or perhaps you're a small business owner searching for ways to diversify your income streams. Guess what? You're also in the right place. With affiliate marketing, you can recommend products that complement your current offerings, adding value for your customers and additional revenue for your business.

You might be a stay-at-home parent, a retiree, a student, or a full-time worker looking for a side hustle. It doesn't matter. Affiliate marketing doesn't discriminate. It doesn't care about your age, your educational background, your current job, or where you're from. All it requires is a willingness to learn, a readiness to act, and a touch of patience.

In this guide, you'll find a wealth of knowledge designed to take you from where you are now, whatever your starting point, to where you want to be — a successful affiliate marketer generating a healthy stream of passive income. So, whether you're just starting out or you're looking to take your online money-making activities to the next level, this book is for you.

How to Use This Book

This book isn't a casual read for a lazy Sunday afternoon. It's a comprehensive guide, a road map if you will, designed to be actioned upon. It's not enough to just read this book — you need to use it. And here's how.

Think of each chapter as a milestone on your affiliate marketing journey. Each one builds on the previous, layering knowledge and skills in a logical and accessible way. We'll start with the basics, ensuring you have a firm understanding of what affiliate marketing is and how it works. Then we'll gradually dive deeper, exploring everything from setting your affiliate marketing goals and building your online presence, to choosing affiliate programs, creating content, promoting your products, and so much more.

As you progress through this guide, we encourage you to take notes, to reflect, to ask questions. Use the practical tips and strategies provided in each chapter to take action – whether it's setting up your website, applying to an affiliate program, writing your first product review, or optimizing your SEO.

Every so often, pause and review what you've learned. Go back and revisit previous chapters if needed. This isn't a race. It's a journey. And every journey moves at its own pace. The key is to keep moving forward, one step at a time.

In this guide, you'll also find real-world case studies that offer a behind-the-scenes look at successful affiliate marketers. These aren't just stories – they're lessons, inspiration, motivation. Use them to learn, to get ideas, and to see what's possible.

At the end of the day, this book is a tool. It's here to help you build your affiliate marketing business and achieve your financial goals. But just like any tool, it's most effective when used correctly. So, take this guide, absorb its lessons, take action on its advice, and watch as you transform from an affiliate marketing beginner into a passive income hero. Your journey starts now.

Chapter 1: Understanding Affiliate Marketing

History and Evolution of Affiliate Marketing

To truly appreciate and understand the world of affiliate marketing, we need to take a stroll down memory lane. By looking at the history and evolution of this vibrant industry, we can better understand its future and the role we'll play in it.

Affiliate marketing, in its simplest form, dates back long before the advent of the internet. In the traditional marketplace, referrals have always been a powerful marketing tool. Think of a local shopkeeper recommending a tailor down the road, or a barber suggesting a particular brand of hair tonic. These are all primitive forms of affiliate marketing. The difference today is the scale and scope enabled by the power of the internet.

Our journey into the history of modern affiliate marketing starts in the late 1980s. A visionary entrepreneur named William J. Tobin was at the helm of a company called PC Flowers & Gifts. Recognizing the untapped potential of the digital space, Tobin launched the first affiliate program, which allowed other websites to link to his online store and earn a commission for any resulting sales.

Though relatively rudimentary by today's standards, this groundbreaking initiative provided a blueprint for future affiliate marketing models.

As the 1990s rolled in, the internet was becoming more and more accessible to the average household. Sensing an opportunity, companies began to explore ways to leverage this exciting new platform. One such company was Amazon.

In 1996, Amazon introduced its own affiliate program, known as Amazon Associates. This program enabled anyone with a website to sign up, promote Amazon's vast array of products, and earn a commission on any sales generated through their affiliate links. The simplicity and accessibility of Amazon's program set the stage for its resounding success, causing a ripple effect throughout the online business world. Affiliate marketing was now officially on the map, and it was here to stay.

Over the following years, the affiliate marketing industry grew and evolved rapidly, hand in hand with advancements in internet technology. As more people got online and e-commerce exploded, the opportunity for affiliates also expanded.

The rise of search engines like Google in the late 90s and early 2000s revolutionized how users navigated the internet. This opened up new strategies for affiliates, such as search engine optimization (SEO) and pay-per-click (PPC) advertising. Affiliates could now optimize their content to appear in search results, driving more traffic to their websites and, consequently, their affiliate links.

Social media platforms started gaining momentum in the mid-2000s, offering yet another avenue for affiliate marketers. Facebook, Twitter, Instagram, and later platforms like Pinterest and TikTok, became fertile ground for promoting affiliate products. Influencers with large followings could earn hefty commissions by endorsing products to their audiences.

The advent of smartphones and mobile internet brought about a new phase in the evolution of affiliate marketing. People were now accessing the internet from anywhere and everywhere, providing affiliates with even more opportunities to reach potential customers.

In the past decade, technologies like AI and machine learning have further refined affiliate marketing strategies.

Tools for data analysis, customer behavior prediction, and personalized advertising have made affiliate marketing more targeted and effective than ever before.

Today, we find ourselves in a thriving, dynamic industry that's continuously evolving. From its humble beginnings to its current status as a billion-dollar industry, affiliate marketing has proven to be a lucrative and accessible venture for millions of individuals and businesses worldwide.

As we stand on the brink of new developments in technology, such as VR and blockchain, we can only imagine what the future holds for affiliate marketing. One thing is for sure, though: affiliate marketing will continue to adapt, grow, and offer opportunities for anyone willing to learn and seize them. It's a vibrant journey that we're all a part of, and the journey is just as rewarding as the destination.

How Affiliate Marketing Works

Now that we have a bit of historical context under our belts, it's time to dive into the nuts and bolts of how affiliate marketing actually works. If you've ever wondered about the process that turns a click on your website into a deposit in your bank account, this section is for you.

In its most basic form, affiliate marketing is a straightforward process involving three key parties: the merchant, the affiliate (which would be you), and the customer. Let's unpack each of these roles and how they interact in the affiliate marketing ecosystem.

1. The Merchant

This is the company or individual that creates the product or service being promoted. A merchant can be a large multinational corporation like Apple or Amazon, a smaller business such as an Etsy shop owner, or even an individual, like a self-published author selling their eBooks. What's essential to understand here is that anyone who has a product or service and is willing to let others promote it in exchange for a commission can be a merchant in the affiliate marketing world.

Merchants see the value in affiliate marketing because it offers a 'pay for performance' model. Rather than sinking money into upfront advertising costs with no guarantee of a return, merchants pay affiliates only when their promotional efforts result in a sale. This setup minimizes risk for the merchant while increasing their product or service's visibility to potential customers they might not have been able to reach otherwise.

2. The Affiliate

This is where you come into the picture. As an affiliate, you'll be promoting the merchant's products or services. You could be running a blog, hosting a podcast, managing a YouTube channel, or maintaining a social media account — any platform where you can reach an audience interested in the merchant's offering.

As an affiliate, your role involves more than just plastering affiliate links everywhere and hoping someone will click and make a purchase. It's about building trust with your audience, offering them value, and recommending products or services that can genuinely benefit them. To succeed as an affiliate, you'll need to understand your audience's needs and wants, then match those with relevant products or services. This is a crucial part of the process we'll explore in more depth later in the book.

3. The Customer

The customer is the lifeblood of the affiliate marketing ecosystem. These are the individuals who will see your promotional content, click on your affiliate links, and hopefully, make a purchase. When they do, you'll earn a commission from the merchant.

It's important to remember that while the affiliate marketing process can benefit both the affiliate and the merchant, it must also benefit the customer. As an affiliate, your role is not just to make sales; it's to help customers solve problems, fulfill needs, or satisfy desires. If you can do this while maintaining their trust and providing value, you'll be well on your way to success as an affiliate marketer.

So, how does all of this come together in practice? It all starts when you, as an affiliate, join an affiliate program run by a merchant. Once accepted into the program, you'll be given unique affiliate links that track any sales coming from your promotional efforts.

You'll then use these links in your content, whether that's a blog post, a social media update, an email newsletter, or a YouTube video. When a customer clicks on your affiliate link, a cookie is stored on their device. This cookie allows the merchant's affiliate system to track the customer's actions and attribute any sales to you.

If the customer makes a purchase, the merchant's affiliate system will record it and attribute a commission to your account. The specifics of this process can vary depending on the affiliate program's terms, but the core principle remains the same.

Affiliate marketing may seem complex on the surface, but at its core, it's a simple and elegant system. It's a symbiotic relationship between merchant, affiliate, and customer that, when executed properly, can bring value to all parties involved. And as we'll explore in the upcoming chapters, it's a system that's ripe with opportunities for those willing to put in the effort and learn the ropes. So buckle up, because our journey into the world of affiliate marketing is just getting started!

Various Types of Affiliate Marketing

Affiliate marketing isn't a monolith. There are numerous ways to approach it, each with its unique opportunities, challenges, and nuances. This diversity is one of the industry's key strengths, offering flexibility and the potential for you to carve out your own niche based on your interests, skills, and available resources. Let's delve deeper into some of the most popular types of affiliate marketing to give you a sense of the possibilities.

1. Blogging

This type of affiliate marketing involves creating a blog and building an audience around a particular topic or niche. Once you have an audience that trusts your opinion and advice, you can recommend products and services related to your niche. This can take the form of dedicated product reviews, "best of" lists, tutorials that involve the use of certain products, and subtle mentions within relevant blog posts. Successful affiliate marketing via blogging typically involves a mix of valuable, engaging content and strategic product promotion.

2. Social Media Marketing

In this type, affiliates leverage their following on social media platforms to promote products and earn commissions. This could be Instagram influencers showcasing a product in their posts or stories, YouTubers mentioning a product during their videos, or Pinterest users creating pins that lead to affiliate products. The key here is authenticity and relevance – social media users can usually tell when an endorsement is forced or irrelevant, so it's crucial to promote products that genuinely fit your brand and audience.

3. Email Marketing

This involves building an email list and promoting products through email campaigns. An affiliate might offer a free eBook, course, or other valuable resource in exchange for a visitor's email address. Once the visitor is on the affiliate's email list, the affiliate can send promotional emails recommending products. Email marketing allows for a more personal, direct connection with your audience, which can often lead to high conversion rates if done correctly.

4. YouTube Marketing

YouTube offers a powerful platform for affiliate marketing. Affiliates can create videos reviewing products, showcasing how to use a product, or comparing different products. Your affiliate links can go in the video description or, in some cases, within the video content itself. With video content booming and YouTube being the second-largest search engine, this method holds a lot of potential.

5. Influencer Marketing

Influencer marketing involves influencers or individuals who have built a large following on a social media platform using their influence to recommend products. They might post an Instagram story using a product, tweet about their love for a particular service, or create a sponsored YouTube video showcasing a product. Brands often reach out to influencers with free products or financial incentives to get them to endorse the brand's offerings.

6. Coupon and Deal Sites

These sites focus on promoting discount codes, special deals, and offers, earning a commission for any sales made through their links. Consumers often visit these sites when they're ready to make a purchase, looking for the best deal, which can lead to high conversion rates.

7. Content Review Sites

These websites center around comprehensive product reviews, comparisons, and "best-of" lists. They're especially popular in industries like tech, beauty, fitness, and more. By providing thorough, in-depth information about products, these sites can often convince readers to purchase through their affiliate links.

8. Niche-specific Sites

These are sites focused around a specific niche, promoting products that are particularly relevant to their target audience. This could be anything from a website about vegan skincare products to a blog about smart home gadgets.

Remember, there's no one-size-fits-all in affiliate marketing. The best approach often involves a mix of these methods, tailored to fit your unique strengths and audience. The beauty of affiliate marketing is that it's flexible and adaptable to your circumstances, preferences, and goals. As we proceed, we'll be taking a closer look at these strategies and how you can apply them to build a successful affiliate marketing business.

Benefits and Challenges of Affiliate Marketing

Like any business venture, affiliate marketing comes with its own set of benefits and challenges. Understanding these can provide you with a balanced perspective and help you make informed decisions as you embark on your affiliate marketing journey.

Benefits of Affiliate Marketing

Low Startup Costs: Unlike traditional businesses that require significant capital to start, affiliate marketing can be launched with a relatively modest budget. All you really need is a website (or a social media profile) and an internet connection. There are even plenty of free resources available to help you get started.

No Need for Product Creation or Inventory: As an affiliate marketer, your role is to connect potential customers with the products they're looking for. You're not responsible for creating these products or managing inventory. This aspect significantly reduces the financial risk and logistical hassles involved in running a business.

Passive Income Potential: Perhaps one of the most attractive aspects of affiliate marketing is its potential to generate passive income. Once you have set up your affiliate links in your content, you can potentially continue to earn income from them for as long as the content remains relevant and accessible. This isn't to say that affiliate marketing doesn't require work—it does, especially in the beginning. However, the potential for passive income is certainly a draw.

Work From Anywhere: Affiliate marketing is a digital venture, meaning you can do it from anywhere in the world that has an internet connection. This flexibility can offer an improved work-life balance and a lifestyle that wouldn't be possible with a typical 9-5 job.

Scalability: With affiliate marketing, your earning potential isn't capped. You're not trading hours for dollars. Instead, the more effective your affiliate marketing strategies are, the more you can potentially earn. There are affiliates out there making a few hundred dollars a month, and there are those making tens of thousands or even hundreds of thousands.

Challenges of Affiliate Marketing

Building an Audience: This is perhaps the most significant challenge new affiliate marketers face. Before you can start earning a substantial income from affiliate marketing, you need to build an audience that trusts your recommendations. This requires creating high-quality content, optimizing for search engines, and promoting your platform.

Earning Trust: Consumers are becoming increasingly savvy about affiliate marketing, and many are wary of content that seems overly promotional or insincere. Earning your audience's trust—and keeping it—is crucial. This means being transparent about your affiliate relationships, only promoting products you believe in, and always prioritizing your audience's needs over making a quick buck.

Market Saturation: There's a lot of competition in the world of affiliate marketing. Many popular niches are highly saturated, with many affiliates vying for the attention of the same audience. Standing out requires creativity, uniqueness, and a lot of effort.

Dependence on Merchant: As an affiliate, you're largely at the mercy of the merchant or affiliate program you've chosen to partner with. Changes in their policies, commission structure, or product offerings can have a significant impact on your income.

SEO Challenges: Search engine optimization (SEO) is crucial for affiliate marketers, as ranking higher in search results can lead to more traffic and conversions. However, SEO is a complex field that's always evolving, and achieving high rankings can be a significant challenge.

Affiliate marketing is an exciting field with significant potential rewards, but it's not a get-rich-quick scheme. It requires effort, patience, and a willingness to learn. If you're willing to face these challenges head-on and put in the necessary work, the benefits can be well worth it. This guide will equip you with the knowledge and strategies you need to overcome these challenges and succeed in your affiliate marketing journey. Now that we've laid the groundwork, it's time to delve deeper into the intricacies of affiliate marketing and start building your path to success.

Chapter 2: The Mechanics of Affiliate Marketing

The Role of Merchants, Affiliates, and Customers

In the affiliate marketing ecosystem, three pivotal roles make the process work seamlessly: the merchant, the affiliate, and the customer. Each player brings unique value to the table, creating a system that, when well-executed, can generate a lucrative income stream for affiliates and drive significant sales for merchants.

Merchant: At the heart of the affiliate marketing process is the merchant. The merchant is the creator or owner of the product or service that the affiliate will be promoting.

They could be a multinational conglomerate or a small, home-based entrepreneur. Whether it's physical goods, digital products, or online services, if they have something to sell, they can use affiliate marketing to increase their sales.

The merchant's role isn't passive, though. Apart from providing the product or service, they are also in charge of setting up the affiliate program, deciding on the commission structure, providing marketing materials (like banners, photos, or product data feeds), tracking affiliate sales, and paying out the affiliates.

Their job also involves maintaining the quality of their products or services. After all, the success of an affiliate marketing strategy heavily depends on the value that customers perceive. If the customers are unhappy with their purchase, it may negatively impact the affiliate's reputation as well. Thus, it's in the merchant's best interest to ensure they deliver a high-quality offering that meets customer expectations.

Affiliate: As an affiliate, you act as a bridge between the merchant and the customer. Affiliates can be individuals like bloggers, YouTubers, or influencers, or they can be entire companies. Their main goal is to promote a merchant's product or service to their audience.

Affiliates do this by creating engaging content that seamlessly integrates the merchant's offerings. The content could be a blog post reviewing the product, a tutorial video on how to use it, a social media post showcasing it, an email newsletter featuring it, or any other form of content that can include affiliate links.

But the role of an affiliate extends beyond just inserting links into their content. They need to build a trustworthy relationship with their audience. They need to understand their audience's needs and wants, and how the products they're promoting can address those. They need to offer genuine value and quality content that keeps their audience engaged and coming back for more.

At the same time, affiliates need to keep abreast of the latest trends and changes in their niche. They need to continually optimize their marketing strategy to maximize their conversion rates and overall success.

Customer: Last but not least, the customers are the end consumers of the product or service. They're the ones who click on the affiliate's link and make a purchase from the merchant's site.

Customers are crucial to the affiliate marketing process. Without them, there are no sales, no commissions, and therefore, no affiliate marketing. They are the driving force behind the revenue generated through this marketing strategy.

The customers may not even realize they're a part of an affiliate marketing system. Whether they know it or not doesn't affect their role in the process. However, it's essential for both the merchant and the affiliate to maintain transparency and let the customer know if an affiliate link is being used.

These three roles work together to make affiliate marketing possible. Understanding each role's function is key to navigating the affiliate marketing landscape successfully. As you progress in your affiliate marketing journey, remember the value that each of these components brings to the table and how you can effectively optimize your role as an affiliate. The more effectively you can communicate with merchants and customers, the more successful your affiliate marketing efforts will be.

The Affiliate Marketing Lifecycle

The affiliate marketing lifecycle is a series of steps that captures the customer's journey from their initial interaction with your content to the completion of a sale. It's a process that encompasses not only the customer's actions but also your activities as an affiliate and the merchant's role. Understanding this lifecycle is crucial to grasp how affiliate marketing works, helping you identify where to focus your efforts for the highest impact.

Here's a detailed breakdown of the affiliate marketing lifecycle:

Merchant Provides Affiliate Materials: At the start of the lifecycle, the merchant needs to have an affiliate program set up. This program includes the creation of unique affiliate links for each affiliate and may also involve providing marketing assets like banners, product images, or sample copy. The merchant also sets up the commission structure, which determines how much affiliates will earn from each sale.

Affiliate Content Creation: Once the affiliate has joined the merchant's program and received their unique affiliate links, it's time for content creation. This phase involves creating engaging, informative, and persuasive content that promotes the merchant's products or services effectively. This content could take the form of blog posts, social media posts, YouTube videos, email newsletters, or any other medium that resonates with the affiliate's audience.

Customer Interaction: The next phase is when potential customers engage with your content. This could be when they read your blog post, watch your video, or see your social media update. The goal of this interaction is to provide them with valuable information and gently guide them towards making a purchase decision.

Click on Affiliate Link: If your content successfully arouses interest in the product or service, the customer will click on the affiliate link embedded within. This link will redirect them to the merchant's site, where they can learn more about the product or proceed to purchase.

Cookie Tracking: When the customer clicks on your affiliate link, a cookie is stored on their browser. This cookie tracks any purchases the customer makes on the merchant's site within a certain period, known as the cookie life. Even if the customer leaves the site and returns later to make a purchase, the sale will still be attributed to you, thanks to the cookie.

Customer Makes a Purchase: The ultimate goal is for the customer to complete a purchase on the merchant's site. If your promotional efforts have been successful and the product or service aligns with the customer's needs or wants, they'll finalize the transaction.

Merchant Tracks the Sale: Once the customer makes a purchase, it's up to the merchant to track the sale. Using the affiliate program's tracking software, they can determine which affiliate link led to the sale.

Affiliate Receives a Commission: The final step in the lifecycle is the affiliate receiving a commission for the sale. The merchant pays this commission according to the agreed-upon structure, usually a percentage of the sale amount.

By understanding the lifecycle, you can identify key touchpoints where you can influence the process. For example, you can optimize your content to better engage potential customers or experiment with different call-to-action placements to increase the chances of customers clicking your affiliate link. The affiliate marketing lifecycle is a roadmap that helps you understand how the system works and where you fit into the larger picture. It's the guide you need to navigate your way to affiliate marketing success.

Understanding Affiliate Links and Cookies

Affiliate links and cookies are fundamental elements of affiliate marketing. They are the digital glue that connects the merchant, the affiliate, and the customer, ensuring the right people get credit where credit is due. Understanding how these elements work is essential to mastering affiliate marketing.

Affiliate Links

What are Affiliate Links?: An affiliate link is a unique URL that includes the affiliate's ID or username. This link is used in the affiliate's content to direct their audience to the merchant's product or service. When the audience clicks on the link and makes a purchase, the affiliate gets a commission.

How do Affiliate Links Work?: When you sign up for an affiliate program, the merchant will provide you with a unique affiliate link. This link is special because it's tagged with your unique ID. When a customer clicks on your affiliate link, that ID is passed along to the merchant's site, allowing them to track that the visitor came from your site.

Using Affiliate Links: As an affiliate, you can use these links in a variety of ways. You can incorporate them into your blog posts, social media posts, email newsletters, or even YouTube video descriptions. It's essential to use these links wisely, integrating them naturally into your content and only promoting products or services that align with your audience's interests and needs.

Cookies

What are Cookies?: In the world of affiliate marketing, a cookie is a small piece of data that is stored on the customer's browser when they click on an affiliate link. This cookie tracks the customer's activities and sends this information back to the merchant's site.

How do Cookies Work in Affiliate Marketing?: When a customer clicks on your affiliate link, a cookie is created and stored on their browser. This cookie contains your unique affiliate ID and a timestamp of when the cookie was created. So, if the customer makes a purchase from the merchant's site, the cookie sends your affiliate ID back to the merchant, letting them know that you referred the customer.

Importance of Cookie Duration: The cookie's duration or "cookie life" is a crucial aspect to consider when joining an affiliate program. Cookie life refers to how long a cookie will stay on the customer's browser after they click your affiliate link. If the customer makes a purchase within this period, you will receive a commission. Cookie lifetimes can vary significantly, from 24 hours to 30, 60, or even 90 days. Some programs even offer "lifetime" cookies that don't expire.

So, in summary, affiliate links and cookies are what make it possible for you as an affiliate to get credit for the customers you refer to the merchant. Understanding these tools not only helps you navigate the technical aspects of affiliate marketing but also assists in evaluating which affiliate programs are likely to be the most rewarding. When choosing an affiliate program, pay close attention to how their affiliate links and cookies work, particularly cookie duration, as it directly affects your potential earnings.

Payment and Commission Structures

When it comes to earning money with affiliate marketing, understanding payment and commission structures is vital. These terms dictate how much you'll earn from your efforts, and recognizing the different structures out there can help you choose the most lucrative affiliate programs that align with your goals.

Payment Models

There are typically three primary types of payment models in affiliate marketing:

Pay Per Sale (PPS): This is the most common payment model. As an affiliate, you earn a commission every time a customer you referred completes a purchase. The commission is usually a percentage of the sale, but it could also be a fixed amount.

Pay Per Lead (PPL): With this model, you earn money each time a customer completes a specific action, such as filling out a form, signing up for a newsletter, or registering for a free trial. These actions are often referred to as "conversions."

Pay Per Click (PPC): This model rewards you every time a customer clicks on your affiliate link and is redirected to the merchant's website. The commission for this model is typically lower because no purchase or conversion is required.

Commission Structures

The commission structures can vary greatly from one affiliate program to another. Here are the main types of commission structures you'll encounter:

Percentage-Based Commissions: This is the most common structure, where you earn a certain percentage of the sale. For example, if the commission rate is 10% and you refer a sale of $100, you'd earn $10.

Fixed Rate Commissions: Here, you earn a set amount for each sale, regardless of the sale price. This structure can be advantageous if the products or services you're promoting have a low cost but high conversion rate.

Tiered Commissions: With this structure, your commission rate increases as you refer more sales. For instance, you might earn a 5% commission on your first 100 sales, 10% on sales 101-200, and so on.

Recurring Commissions: Some affiliate programs offer recurring commissions for subscription-based products or services. This means you'll continue to earn a commission for as long as the customer you referred stays subscribed.

Cookie Life: While not technically a commission structure, the cookie life can affect your earnings.

As we discussed earlier, the cookie life refers to the period in which a sale can be credited to you after a customer clicks on your affiliate link. A longer cookie life usually means more opportunities to earn commissions.

When choosing an affiliate program, make sure to consider the payment model and commission structure. These elements will have a direct impact on your earning potential. In some cases, a high commission rate might be attractive, but if the product's price is low or the conversion rate is poor, you might earn more from a program with a lower commission but a higher conversion rate or price.

Always remember, your affiliate marketing journey is not just about making quick money. It's about building a sustainable, long-term business that provides value to your audience. Therefore, choose affiliate programs with products or services that align with your audience's needs and wants, even if they might not have the highest paying commission structure. The trust and loyalty you'll gain from your audience will be worth far more in the long run.

Chapter 3: Setting Your Affiliate Marketing Goals

The Importance of Clear Goals

There's an age-old saying that if you don't know where you're going, you'll probably end up somewhere else. It's a simple but profound statement, and when it comes to affiliate marketing, or any venture really, it hits the nail right on the head.

When you first step into the world of affiliate marketing, it's like standing at the edge of a vast forest. There are countless paths leading in all directions, and it's easy to feel overwhelmed and lost. This is where clear goals step in. They act like a compass, guiding you through this forest, helping you navigate and choose the right path.

Imagine you're a ship sailing on the open sea. Goals are your destination, the island you're aiming for. Without them, you'll just be drifting, pushed around by the winds and currents. You might eventually land somewhere, but will it be where you wanted? Without a clear destination in mind, it's impossible to chart a course and steer the ship accordingly.

That's the primary reason why clear goals are so critical. They give you direction. They allow you to plot a course and steer your affiliate marketing ship towards your chosen destination.

But there's more to it. Goals also provide a measuring stick for your progress. Say you've set a goal to make $1000 a month from your affiliate marketing efforts within the first year. This goal allows you to track your progress over time. You can see if you're on track, ahead, or falling behind. If you're falling behind, you can reassess and figure out what you need to do to catch up.

This ability to measure progress is invaluable. It not only keeps you informed about how you're doing but also provides motivation. Each step towards your goal, each dollar you earn, is a small victory. It's confirmation that you're on the right track, that your efforts are bearing fruit. This can be incredibly motivating, especially when the going gets tough, as it inevitably will.

Goals also help you maintain focus. In the world of affiliate marketing, there are countless opportunities and avenues to explore. While this is generally a good thing, it can also lead to what's known as "shiny object syndrome." This is when you constantly jump from one opportunity to another, always chasing the next big thing, but never sticking with one long enough to see real results. Clear, well-defined goals can help you avoid this trap. They keep your eyes on the prize, helping you stay focused and committed to your chosen path.

Finally, and perhaps most importantly, goals empower you. They put you in the driver's seat of your journey. You're no longer at the mercy of the winds and currents, drifting aimlessly. You're in control, steering your ship towards your chosen destination.

Setting goals doesn't guarantee success, but it greatly increases your chances. So, take some time to reflect on what you want to achieve with affiliate marketing. Set clear, realistic goals that align with your personal and financial aspirations. Write them down, keep them somewhere you can regularly see, and remind yourself of them often.

In the following sections, we'll delve deeper into how to define your niche and set SMART goals that will propel your affiliate marketing journey. You'll soon see how these critical steps provide a strong foundation and a clear direction for your future success.

Defining Your Niche

Now, let's talk about niches. You're probably wondering, "What's a niche, and why does it matter?" A niche, my friend, is like your territory in the vast landscape of the internet, and it's a fundamental aspect of affiliate marketing.

Think of the internet as a colossal marketplace, filled with stalls selling all sorts of products and services. Each stall caters to a specific audience looking for a particular type of product. This is what we call a niche: a specific segment of a market.

Choosing your niche is a bit like deciding what type of stall you want to set up in this marketplace. Are you going to sell handmade jewelry, vintage vinyl records, or maybe organic skincare products? Your choice will determine who you're targeting and the type of content you'll be creating. Essentially, it's the space you choose to occupy in the market, and it guides the direction of your affiliate marketing efforts.

One of the biggest mistakes beginners make in affiliate marketing is trying to appeal to everyone. But the truth is, if you're trying to talk to everyone, you're effectively talking to no one. That's why having a specific niche is so crucial. It allows you to tailor your content, products, and services to a defined audience. By doing this, you can stand out from the crowd and build a loyal following.

But how do you choose your niche? First, think about your interests and passions. This is important because affiliate marketing is not a get-rich-quick scheme. It takes time and effort, and it's much easier to invest that time and effort into something you're passionate about.

Imagine trying to create a blog or social media account about something you have zero interest in. Sounds dreadful, right? Now imagine doing that for a topic you love. That's a whole different ball game. You'll enjoy the process, and that passion will shine through in your content, making it more engaging and authentic.

Next, consider your knowledge and expertise. What are you good at? What topics do people often ask your advice on? Your expertise not only lends credibility to your affiliate marketing efforts but also allows you to provide value to your audience.

Finally, consider market demand. Even if you're passionate about a topic and have a lot of knowledge in it, if there's no demand for it in the market, it might be challenging to make money from it. Do some research to see if people are interested in your niche and willing to spend money on it.

Look at what's already out there. Are there other blogs, social media accounts, or websites in the same niche? Are there affiliate products available that you can promote? These can all be indications of a profitable niche.

Also, consider the future potential of your niche. Is it a passing trend, or does it have staying power? Remember, affiliate marketing is a long game.

You want to choose a niche that will still be relevant and profitable a few years down the line.

Choosing a niche is a crucial step in your affiliate marketing journey. It's like choosing your path in the forest or setting the course for your ship. It might seem a bit daunting at first, but take your time. Reflect on your interests, passions, skills, and the market demand. And remember, you're not locked into your choice forever. As you learn and grow, you might find that your niche evolves with you. That's completely fine, and it's part of the journey.

Once you've found your niche, you're ready for the next step: setting SMART goals. But more on that in the next section. For now, let's focus on discovering the unique niche that will pave the way for your success in affiliate marketing.

Setting SMART Goals

Alright, now that we've talked about the importance of goals and defining your niche, it's time to dive into the specifics of setting goals - and not just any goals, but SMART goals.

You might have heard of this acronym before, and you're about to hear it again because it's a game-changer. SMART stands for Specific, Measurable, Achievable, Relevant, and Time-bound. Let's break that down, shall we?

Specific: Your goals need to be clear and well-defined. Vague or generalized goals are a no-go. They lack direction and often lead to frustration because you're never quite sure when you've achieved them. Instead of saying "I want to earn more money," say "I want to earn $1000 a month from affiliate marketing." Now that's specific!

Measurable: A goal without a measurable outcome is like a sports competition without a scoreboard or scorekeeper. Numbers are a friend to goals; they provide a concrete way to see if you're getting closer to your goal or not. With the same example, $1000 a month is something you can track and measure.

Achievable: It's good to shoot for the stars, but don't set goals that are so high they only lead to discouragement. Set goals that challenge you, but are still within the realms of possibility considering your resources and constraints. If you're a beginner in affiliate marketing, for instance, setting a goal to earn a million dollars in your first month might be a stretch.

Relevant: Your goals should align with your long-term plans and aspirations. If you're embarking on affiliate marketing to create a passive income stream, then your goals should reflect that. It's about ensuring your goal fits with your broader plan.

Time-bound: Goals need a timeline. Without a deadline, there's no sense of urgency, and your motivation could dwindle. Having a time limit creates a sense of urgency that can motivate you to get started. For example, aim to hit that $1000 monthly earning within your first year.

So, a SMART goal for a beginner in affiliate marketing could be something like this: "I want to earn $1000 per month from my affiliate marketing business within one year."

But why are SMART goals so beneficial? Well, they force you to think through your goals carefully. They make you get clear on what you want, why you want it, and how you're going to achieve it. This clarity is invaluable. It guides your actions, keeps you on track, and significantly increases your chances of success.

Plus, SMART goals are motivating. They give you a clear target to aim for, and there's nothing quite as satisfying as hitting a target.

Remember, though, that while setting SMART goals is a powerful tool, it's not a magic wand. It won't automatically lead to success. You still need to put in the effort, take consistent action, and keep learning and adjusting along the way.

In the following section, we'll talk about how to translate your SMART goals into a winning strategy. But for now, spend some time crafting your own SMART goals. Remember, they should be specific, measurable, achievable, relevant, and time-bound. Make them count, and make them work for you!

From Goals to Strategy

Setting goals is one thing, but without a solid plan, they're like stars in the night sky - beautiful to look at, but a bit out of reach. That's where strategy comes in.

When I say 'strategy,' I know it might sound a little heavy-duty, like we're planning a military operation or a chess tournament. But, in essence, a strategy is just a detailed plan, a roadmap that will guide you from where you are now (point A: affiliate marketing newbie) to where you want to be (point B: passive income hero).

Think of it like going on a road trip. You know your destination, but you also need to know which route you're taking, where you'll stop along the way, and what you'll need to bring with you. Your strategy is your road trip plan.

First off, know your audience. Who are you trying to reach? What do they need or want? The better you understand your audience, the better you can create content that resonates with them, and the more likely they are to trust your recommendations and click on your affiliate links. This is where choosing a niche comes into play.

Next, choose the right affiliate products or services. They should be relevant to your niche and audience. Also, consider their quality and reputation. Your audience trusts you, so don't break that trust by promoting inferior products or services.

Then, plan your content. What kind of content will you create? Blog posts? Videos? Podcasts? Whatever you choose, your content should be engaging, valuable, and build trust with your audience. It should also be optimized for search engines so that people can find it. And of course, it should naturally incorporate your affiliate links.

Another key part of your strategy is promotion. Creating great content is only half the battle. You also need to get it in front of people. You could have the best content in the world, but if no one sees it, it won't help you reach your goals. So, plan how you'll promote your content. Will you use social media? Email marketing? Paid ads?

Don't forget about tracking and analysis. What gets measured gets managed, as they say. Regularly check on your progress. Are you getting closer to your goals? What's working well, and what's not? Use analytics tools to gather data, and use this information to refine and adjust your strategy.

Lastly, be prepared to learn and adapt. The online landscape changes fast. New trends emerge, algorithms update, and audience behaviors shift. Stay informed about these changes and be ready to tweak your strategy as needed. This isn't a set-and-forget kind of deal.

A well-thought-out strategy is like a compass. It keeps you on course and helps you navigate the twists and turns of your affiliate marketing journey. Remember, your strategy should be flexible, not rigid. It's a guide, not a rule book.

Now that you've set your SMART goals and laid out your strategy, you're well on your way to becoming a passive income hero. In the next chapter, we'll dive into the practical side of things: building your online presence. But for now, take a moment to pat yourself on the back. You're laying a solid foundation, and that's something to be proud of.

So, buckle up and get ready for the ride. With your goals as your destination and your strategy as your roadmap, there's no limit to what you can achieve. Let's turn those affiliate marketing dreams into reality!

Chapter 4: Building Your Online Presence

Creating Your Website

Alright, it's time to roll up your sleeves and dive into the nitty-gritty of creating your website, the lighthouse that will guide your audience through the turbulent sea of the internet. I promise, it's not as hard as it sounds, and it can even be a whole lot of fun. So, let's buckle up, get our creative gears turning, and jump right in.

The first thing you need is a domain name. This is your website's address on the internet, and it's what people will type into their browsers to find your site. Choosing a domain name can be a creative endeavor. You want something that's easy to remember, reflects your brand, and resonates with your target audience. It's your first impression, your digital handshake, if you will.

Once you've picked out your perfect domain name, it's time to select a hosting provider. Your hosting provider is the company that stores your website's files and makes them accessible on the internet. There are many factors to consider when choosing a hosting provider, like reliability, speed, customer support, and of course, cost. Think of it as finding a home for your website, so you want a host that's secure, speedy, and doesn't leave you hanging when you need help.

Now comes the exciting part—designing your website. Today's website builders make it easy to create a site that looks professional and is easy to navigate, even for beginners. You'll be able to choose from a variety of templates, customize the colors and fonts, and easily add pages and features like a blog, contact form, or online store.

Now, let's chat about the structure of your site. You want it to be user-friendly, so your visitors can easily find what they're looking for. Start with a few essential pages like a home page, about page, and contact page. If you're planning to start a blog (which is a great idea for an affiliate marketing site), you'll also want a blog page where your posts can live.

On your homepage, make it clear who you are, what you do, and who you serve. Your about page is a chance to share your story, why you started your affiliate marketing journey, and why your audience should trust your recommendations.

Your website is also the place where you'll share valuable, relevant content that resonates with your audience. Whether it's blog posts, videos, infographics, or reviews of the products you're promoting, this content is what will attract visitors to your site, keep them coming back, and convince them to click on your affiliate links.

It's essential to keep your website fresh and updated. Regularly adding new content not only keeps your audience engaged but also helps improve your website's visibility in search engines, a concept we'll delve deeper into when we talk about SEO.

Lastly, ensure that your website is mobile-friendly. With more and more people using their smartphones to browse the internet, a website that looks great and functions well on mobile devices is a must.

Creating your website is a big step, but it's also an exciting one. It's your chance to establish your brand, connect with your audience, and start sharing and promoting the products or services you believe in. So don't be daunted by the technical side of things. Embrace the learning curve and enjoy the journey. With each step, you're getting closer to becoming a passive income hero!

Building Your Social Media Presence

Let's flip to the next chapter of our journey. Imagine you've got your fabulous website ready to shine and you're excited to show it off to the world. But how do you get the world to visit your website? That's where building a robust social media presence comes into play. Social media, if done right, can act as a powerful vehicle driving traffic to your website. So, buckle up and let's delve into the realm of likes, shares, and retweets.

At the heart of social media success is the idea of community. It's all about creating relationships and establishing a two-way conversation with your audience. Think of social media as a party. You wouldn't just walk in, shout about your products, and walk out, right? Instead, you'd engage with people, listen to what they're saying, and build genuine relationships. That's exactly what you should be doing on social media.

Begin with choosing the right platforms. With a plethora of social media platforms out there, it might seem tempting to set up shop on all of them. But trust me, you'd rather focus on a few that are most relevant to your audience. Are they more likely to hang out on Instagram or LinkedIn? Is Twitter their thing, or do they prefer Facebook? Look at factors like the age, interests, and location of your audience to make an informed decision.

Once you've picked your platforms, it's time to start posting. But wait, don't just post for the sake of posting. Each post should add value, entertain, educate, or inspire your audience. Also, make sure to maintain a consistent posting schedule. This doesn't mean you need to post every day, but it does mean you need to be regular and consistent with your posts.

To make your life easier, consider using social media management tools that allow you to schedule posts in advance. That way, even on days when you're busy, your social media presence doesn't have to take a hit.

Social media is also a fantastic place to share your blog posts, product reviews, and any other content you create. Each time you publish a new post on your website, share it on your social platforms to drive traffic back to your site.

Don't forget to engage with your audience. Reply to comments, ask questions, start discussions, and show that there's a real person behind the account. Remember the party analogy? It's all about the conversation.

Don't be afraid to show your personality on social media. This is especially important if you're a solopreneur or running a small business. People love connecting with people, not faceless corporations. Be authentic, share a bit about your life and behind-the-scenes stories. It helps to humanize your brand and builds trust with your audience.

Paid social media advertising is another route to consider, but we'll dive deep into that later in the book. For now, just know that it's a powerful way to reach a larger audience and direct more traffic to your website.

In a nutshell, social media is a powerful tool in your affiliate marketing arsenal. It's a place to connect, share, engage, and grow your audience. So, start posting, start engaging, and let's get that party started!

Email Marketing Basics

Alright, we've built a website and started making some noise on social media. Now, let's dive into another crucial aspect of building your online presence - Email Marketing. Yes, you heard it right! Despite all the buzz around social media and SEO, email is far from dead. In fact, it's alive, kicking, and an absolute powerhouse when it comes to driving conversions. So, let's unpack this a bit, shall we?

Let's start with why you need email marketing. Picture this: You've got visitors coming to your website, they look around, and then they leave. The next day, they probably won't even remember your website. But what if you could keep the conversation going even after they've left your site? Enter email marketing.

In its simplest form, email marketing is all about building a list of email addresses (subscribers) and sending them regular emails. These could be updates, newsletters, special offers, or anything else that might interest your audience.

The first step is to collect email addresses, and the best way to do this is by offering something valuable in exchange. This could be a free ebook, a discount code, a valuable piece of content, or anything else that your visitors would be willing to exchange their email addresses for. This is often referred to as a lead magnet. But remember, the goal here is not just to grow your list but to attract the right kind of subscribers - those who are interested in what you have to offer.

Next, you need an email marketing service. This is a software that allows you to manage your email list, send emails, and track your results. There are plenty of options out there, some free and some paid. When choosing one, consider factors like ease of use, features, price, and customer support.

Now, let's talk about the fun part - sending emails. When it comes to email marketing, content is king. It's not just about promoting your products or services, it's about providing value.

Think of your emails as a way to build a relationship with your subscribers, not just as a sales pitch. A mix of informative content, tips, exclusive offers, and personal stories usually works well.

As for frequency, there's no one-size-fits-all answer. It depends on your audience and the kind of content you're sending. However, it's important to maintain a balance. You don't want to flood their inbox and risk being marked as spam, but you also don't want them to forget about you. A good place to start might be once a week, but feel free to experiment and see what works best for your audience.

Another thing to keep in mind is personalization. Most email marketing services allow you to personalize your emails with the subscriber's name or other information. This can go a long way in making your subscribers feel special and valued.

And last but definitely not least, track your results. Most email marketing services provide analytics like open rates, click-through rates, and more. Use this data to understand what's working and what's not, and adjust your strategy accordingly.

In a nutshell, email marketing is all about building and nurturing relationships with your audience. It's a way to keep the conversation going, provide value, and gently guide your subscribers along the path to becoming customers. And the best part? It's completely within your control.

Basics of SEO and SEM

Now that we've covered the importance of creating your website, building your social media presence, and getting started with email marketing, it's time to dive into the exciting world of Search Engine Optimization (SEO) and Search Engine Marketing (SEM). Don't worry, it might sound technical, but I'll break it down so it's as easy to understand as Sunday morning.

Let's kick things off with SEO, which is all about making your website appealing to search engines like Google and Bing. The ultimate goal? To get your website to show up on the first page of search results when someone types in a relevant keyword or phrase. That's because websites on the first page of Google get a whopping 91.5% of all search traffic. So, being on that first page can mean a massive increase in visibility for your affiliate marketing business.

First, let's talk keywords. These are words or phrases that your target audience is likely to type into a search engine. For example, if your affiliate website is about hiking gear, relevant keywords might be 'best hiking boots', 'lightweight tents' or 'waterproof backpacks'. There are plenty of tools out there, like Google Keyword Planner or SEMRush, that can help you identify relevant keywords.

But SEO isn't just about stuffing your content with keywords. Search engines are smarter than that. They want to provide users with high-quality, relevant content. That means your content needs to be well-written, helpful, and relevant to the keywords you're targeting.

Aside from content, another key aspect of SEO is building backlinks, which are links from other websites to yours. In the eyes of search engines, each backlink serves as a vote of confidence in your content. However, not all backlinks are created equal. Those from high-authority websites are worth much more than ones from low-quality sites.

Now, let's move on to SEM. While SEO is all about earning traffic organically, SEM involves buying traffic through paid search listings. This is often done through Pay-Per-Click (PPC) advertising, where you pay each time someone clicks on your ad.

A great place to start with SEM is Google Ads. Here, you can bid on the keywords you want to target. When someone searches for one of those keywords, your ad may appear at the top of the search results. And the best part? You only pay when someone clicks on your ad.

Another part of SEM is retargeting, which allows you to show ads to people who've visited your website but didn't make a purchase or fill out a contact form. This keeps your brand at the top of their minds and increases the chances of them returning to your site.

Both SEO and SEM have their pros and cons. SEO takes time but provides long-lasting results, while SEM can bring in traffic quickly but comes at a cost. For the best results, a combination of both is often the way to go.

It's important to remember that SEO and SEM aren't set-it-and-forget-it tasks. They require continuous effort and adjustments based on changes in search engine algorithms, competition, and your own website's performance. But don't let that discourage you. With time, patience, and a willingness to learn, you can leverage both to significantly boost your affiliate marketing business.

So there you have it - SEO and SEM in a nutshell! With this knowledge, you're well on your way to boosting your website's visibility and attracting more potential customers. But remember, Rome wasn't built in a day. SEO and SEM take time, so be patient, stay consistent, and the results will follow.

Chapter 5: Selecting the Right Affiliate Programs

Well, isn't this exciting? We're already at the point where we're going to talk about selecting the right affiliate programs! This is a vital step because, let's be honest, not all affiliate programs are created equal. It's like choosing between different types of pizza. Some will have the right balance of cheese and toppings, while others might skimp on the good stuff. So, let's dive right in and learn how to pick the pizza, I mean affiliate program, that suits you best.

Factors to Consider

As I mentioned before, choosing the right affiliate program is somewhat akin to picking out a great pizza. It's got to have the right ingredients that come together to make the perfect slice for your palate. Likewise, the best affiliate program for you is one that meets specific key criteria.

It's the one that fits your niche and business model, aligns with your audience's interests, and offers a fair commission for your marketing efforts. So, let's break this down, shall we?

First and foremost, the relevance to your niche is key. Imagine going to a famous steakhouse and getting served sushi. No matter how delicious it might be, you'd feel confused, right? The same applies to your website and your audience. If your website is all about hiking and outdoor adventures, joining an affiliate program selling beauty products will only serve to confuse your audience and dilute your message. Always go for an affiliate program whose products or services align with your website's niche and can genuinely add value to your audience's lives.

Next, let's talk about the quality of the product or service. Your website's credibility and your audience's trust are at stake here. Picture this: you recommend a product, your audience buys it, but then they find out that it's faulty or doesn't deliver on its promises. Your audience will not only be disappointed, but they'll also question your integrity and the trustworthiness of your recommendations. And once lost, trust is hard to regain. Therefore, you must ensure that whatever you promote is of good quality and provides real value to your audience.

Now let's talk dollars and cents, or rather, commission rates. Different affiliate programs offer different commission rates. Some might offer a whopping 50% commission but on a $10 product. Others might offer a seemingly meager 5% commission, but if it's on a $500 product, you're in for a nice $25 per sale. And then there are those that offer a fixed amount per sale, regardless of the product price. It's essential to run the numbers and see which structure fits your potential traffic volume, conversion rate, and overall profit margin best.

The cookie duration is another factor that needs your attention. Remember when I mentioned cookies earlier? No, not the chocolate chip ones, but the digital kind. Cookies are used in affiliate marketing to track the journey of a customer from your website to the merchant's website. If a customer, who has clicked on your affiliate link, makes a purchase within the cookie duration, you get a commission. Now, these durations can vary greatly among programs – some offer 24 hours, others 30 days, and some even up to 365 days. Generally, the longer the cookie duration, the better your chances of earning a commission.

Finally, there's the reputation and reviews of the affiliate program itself. Let's use our pizza metaphor again. Would you order from a place that has numerous bad reviews about late deliveries and cold pizzas? Probably not. Similarly, you need to do your homework and find out what other affiliates are saying about the program you're considering. Do they pay on time? Do they provide good support? Are there any issues with tracking sales? Online forums, social media groups, and review websites can provide a wealth of information here.

And voila, there you have it – the ingredients for choosing the perfect affiliate program! These factors, when considered carefully, will help you make a well-informed decision and set you on the path to affiliate marketing success. Let's remember, this process is not a race. Take your time, do your homework, and choose wisely. In the next section, we'll discuss how to research potential affiliate programs and delve deeper into the application and approval process.

Researching Potential Affiliate Programs

Alright, let's move onto the fun part, kind of like a detective's work - researching potential affiliate programs.

Picture yourself as a detective, like Sherlock Holmes or Nancy Drew. You've got a magnifying glass in one hand and a notebook in the other. You're ready to uncover the truth about potential affiliate programs. Ok, maybe it's not that dramatic, but hey, research can be fun when you're on a mission to find the best opportunities!

The first place to start your research is with affiliate networks. These are essentially the middlemen that connect merchants who want to sell their products with affiliates (like you!) who want to promote those products. Some of the most popular affiliate networks include ClickBank, CJ Affiliate, and ShareASale. These platforms host thousands of affiliate programs across various niches, making it a great starting point to find potential affiliate programs. Plus, these networks usually provide a wealth of information about each program, including commission rates, cookie duration, and product details, making your detective work a bit easier.

Another method is to conduct a direct search. This can be as simple as typing "[Your Niche] + affiliate program" into your favorite search engine. This method can often reveal some hidden gems that aren't part of the major affiliate networks. However, it may require a bit more digging to find all the details you need.

One important thing you want to check for during your research is the sales page of the product or service. This is the page that your audience will land on after clicking your affiliate link. You want to make sure that this page is compelling, professional, and has a strong call to action. If the sales page is poorly designed or confusing, it could lower your conversion rate, no matter how much traffic you send.

Next up, you'll want to evaluate the product reviews and ratings. This not only gives you a sense of the product's quality but also how it's perceived by its users. Be on the lookout for any common issues or complaints. Remember, your audience's trust is on the line, so it's better to promote products that are well-received by users.

Also, don't forget to consider the support and resources offered by the program. Good affiliate programs provide their affiliates with promotional materials, such as banners, images, and email swipes, and training resources to help you succeed. They also have responsive support teams that are ready to assist you when you need help.

Lastly, consider the payment terms. How and when will you be paid? Some programs pay monthly, others quarterly. Some offer payment via PayPal, while others may use direct bank transfer or check. Make sure that the payment terms align with your needs and preferences.

Remember, your research process should be thorough, but it doesn't need to be stressful. Just like choosing a pizza, you're looking for the best fit for your tastes (or in this case, your business needs). Take your time, gather information, and don't be afraid to ask questions if something isn't clear. This research will form the foundation of your affiliate marketing business, so it's well worth the effort.

So, there we have it, your personal guide to researching affiliate programs! In the next section, we will go into the application process and approval for these programs. Keep that detective hat on; we've got some more sleuthing to do!

Application Process and Approval

Alright, we're on a roll now, aren't we? You've done your detective work and found some fantastic affiliate programs. The next step? Applying to them and getting that coveted approval. So let's dive into it.

You see, becoming an affiliate marketer isn't like walking into a shop and picking up your favorite chocolate bar. There's a process involved, and it involves some patience, diligence, and the willingness to put your best foot forward. So, let's demystify this process.

Application Form: First off, you'll need to fill out an application form. This is where the merchant gets to know a bit about you, your website, your promotional methods, and your target audience. Here, honesty is the best policy. You want to be truthful about your strategies and intentions. After all, this is the start of a potential long-term relationship.

Website Evaluation: Next, most programs will evaluate your website or platform where you plan to promote their products. They are looking for sites that align with their brand, have relevant content, and follow ethical marketing practices. It's a good idea to ensure your website is well-designed, with quality content published regularly. Think of it as preparing your home for some very important guests.

Approval (or not): After reviewing your application, the merchant will either approve or deny your application. If you're approved, great! You're ready to start promoting. If not, don't be disheartened. It's not uncommon for applications to be initially rejected. Use it as a learning opportunity. Reach out to the merchant and ask for feedback on why your application was rejected. Most will be willing to give you some insights, which you can use to improve and reapply.

Now, it might seem a bit daunting, but I assure you it's not as scary as it sounds. In fact, let's talk about some tips to increase your chances of getting approved.

Have a Well-Designed Website: Your website is your portfolio. It's the first impression merchants have of you. Make sure it's a good one. Clean design, quality content, clear navigation, these all matter.

Know Your Audience: Merchants want to know that their products will be promoted to a relevant audience. Be able to articulate who your audience is, what their needs and interests are, and how the merchant's product fits into that picture.

Follow Best Practices: Comply with all legal and ethical guidelines, especially those related to disclosure and privacy. This demonstrates to merchants that you are a serious, professional, and trustworthy partner.

Patience Is Key: This isn't a race. Take your time to research and apply to the programs that best match your brand and audience. It's better to be a part of a few programs that really fit than many that don't.

Communication: Don't be afraid to reach out to the merchant or the affiliate manager if you have questions or need clarification. Good communication can set the foundation for a successful partnership.

The application process might feel a bit like a hurdle, but once you clear it, it's smooth sailing. So, take a deep breath, prepare well, and put your best foot forward. You've got this!

Stay with me, as in the next chapter, we're going to look at creating valuable content. Trust me; you don't want to miss that one. After all, content is the heart of affiliate marketing. Ready to pump some life into your affiliate marketing journey? Let's go!

Chapter 6: Creating Valuable Content

The Importance of Quality Content

Alright, my friends, are you ready to dive into the exciting world of content creation? This chapter is all about creating content that not only sells but also builds trust with your audience.

So, we all know that quality content is the cornerstone of your affiliate marketing success. But what makes content "quality," and why does it matter so much? Grab a cup of coffee (or tea, if you're so inclined) and let's delve a little deeper into this.

The importance of quality content in affiliate marketing cannot be overstated. You know, as humans, we naturally gravitate towards things that add value to our lives, whether it's a useful gadget, an educational course, or a helpful blog post. The same principle applies to your audience. If your content provides them with tangible value, they will keep coming back for more, and this is where the magic happens in affiliate marketing.

Understanding the Value Proposition

Picture this: you have two stores selling the same product at the same price. Store A has salespeople who are knowledgeable, helpful, and enthusiastic. Store B's salespeople, on the other hand, are indifferent, unhelpful, and seem uninterested in the products they're selling. Which store would you choose to buy from? Most likely, Store A, right?

The same principle applies to affiliate marketing. Your content is like the salesperson in our example. If it's high-quality, valuable, and engaging, people are more likely to trust your recommendations and click on your affiliate links. If it's not, well, you can guess what happens.

Building Trust with Your Audience

Trust is another critical factor in affiliate marketing. When people trust you, they're more likely to follow your recommendations. And how do you build trust? You guessed it: through quality content.

The quality of your content reflects on you and your brand. If your content is well-researched, well-written, and provides value, it shows that you're knowledgeable and that you care about your audience. This helps build trust.

On the other hand, if your content is full of errors, lacks depth, or is purely promotional, it can damage your reputation and trustworthiness. So, always aim to create the best content possible.

Driving Traffic and Conversions

Quality content is also key to driving traffic and conversions. When your content is high-quality, people are more likely to share it with their friends, comment on it, and engage with it. This increases your visibility and helps attract more traffic to your site.

Furthermore, high-quality content can help improve your SEO, making your site more visible on search engines and driving more organic traffic.

And when it comes to conversions, quality content can make all the difference. If your content provides value, solves a problem, or answers a question for your audience, they're more likely to trust your recommendations and buy the products you're promoting.

Engagement and Retention

Finally, quality content helps drive engagement and retention. If your content is engaging and provides value, people will spend more time on your site. They're also more likely to return in the future and become loyal followers or customers.

This is particularly important in affiliate marketing, as it's often easier and more cost-effective to retain existing followers or customers than to acquire new ones.

So, as you can see, quality content is vital in affiliate marketing. It's the foundation upon which all your other efforts are built. It helps you build trust with your audience, drive traffic and conversions, and improve engagement and retention.

So, my friend, commit to creating quality content. It might take a little more effort and time, but trust me, it's well worth it. Your audience will thank you, and your affiliate marketing business will flourish.

Alright, that's enough about the importance of quality content for now. Up next, we're going to delve into the art of creating content that sells. Stay tuned, and keep sipping that coffee (or tea)!

Creating Content That Sells

All right, friend, we've had our chat about the importance of quality content, now let's dive into the exciting world of creating content that sells. Yes, you heard right! Not all content is created equal, and if your aim is to make those affiliate commissions, you want to focus on content that doesn't just inform, but persuades and converts. So, buckle up and let's get started!

Painting a Picture with Your Content

When it comes to affiliate marketing, your primary goal is to convince your audience that the product or service you're promoting will solve their problem or fulfill their needs. It's not enough to just list the features or benefits of the product; you need to paint a picture of how the product fits into their lives, how it will make things easier, better, or more enjoyable.

For example, if you're promoting a new kitchen gadget, don't just tell your audience that it's "fast," "efficient," or "easy to use." Instead, describe how it will help them whip up a delicious, healthy dinner for their family in half the time, or how it will make hosting parties a breeze. Create a story that your audience can relate to and see themselves in, and you'll have a much better chance of convincing them to click that affiliate link.

Using Emotional Triggers

Believe it or not, most purchasing decisions aren't based purely on logic; they're driven by emotion. So, to create content that sells, you need to tap into your audience's emotions.

This doesn't mean resorting to manipulation or scare tactics. Instead, it's about understanding your audience's needs, desires, fears, and frustrations, and showing them how the product you're promoting can help address these.

If you can make your audience feel understood and show them that you have a solution to their problem, they're much more likely to trust your recommendation and make a purchase.

Creating a Sense of Urgency

One of the most effective ways to persuade your audience to take action is to create a sense of urgency. This could be by highlighting a limited-time offer, a sale that's about to end, or a product that's in high demand and likely to sell out soon.

Of course, it's crucial to be honest and transparent when doing this. Don't create a false sense of urgency, as this could damage your reputation and trust with your audience.

Incorporating Social Proof

Social proof is another powerful tool for creating content that sells. This could be testimonials, reviews, or case studies showing how others have benefited from the product.

Seeing that others have had a positive experience with the product can help alleviate any doubts or concerns your audience might have, and convince them to give it a try.

Clear and Compelling Call to Actions

Finally, don't forget to include clear and compelling calls to action (CTAs) in your content. Your CTA should tell your audience exactly what action you want them to take, whether it's clicking on an affiliate link, signing up for a newsletter, or leaving a comment.

Remember, your audience won't take action unless you ask them to, so don't be shy about telling them what you want them to do!

Well, there you have it, my friend, the art of creating content that sells. Remember, the key is to understand your audience, tell a compelling story, tap into their emotions, create a sense of urgency, incorporate social proof, and use clear and compelling CTAs.

Sounds like a lot? Don't worry, with practice, it will become second nature. Now, go ahead and start creating that selling content, and watch those affiliate commissions roll in! In the next section, we're going to talk about SEO for affiliate marketing.

SEO for Affiliate Marketing

Search Engine Optimization, or SEO, might sound a bit technical and daunting if you're new to this, but I assure you it's not as complex as you might think. Plus, mastering SEO is like having a superpower in the affiliate marketing world, so it's definitely worth the effort to learn.

Why is SEO Important for Affiliate Marketing?

SEO is essentially the art and science of making your content visible and attractive to search engines, like Google, Bing, or Yahoo. In a sea of billions of web pages, your content is like a tiny island. Without SEO, your island remains invisible and difficult to reach. But with SEO, you essentially build bridges to your island, making it easier for search engines to find it and for users to reach it. In other words, good SEO brings more traffic to your website, and more traffic means more potential clicks on your affiliate links, which translates into more potential commissions.

Keywords: The Building Blocks of SEO

Now, the cornerstone of SEO is keywords. These are the words and phrases that people type into search engines when they're looking for information. Your job as an affiliate marketer is to figure out which keywords your target audience is using and then to include these keywords in your content.

You might be thinking, "But how do I figure out which keywords to use?" Great question! There are a number of free and paid tools out there that can help you with this, such as Google Keyword Planner, SEMrush, or Ahrefs. These tools show you how often a particular keyword is searched for, how much competition there is for that keyword, and even suggest related keywords that you might not have thought of.

On-Page SEO: Making Your Content Search-Engine Friendly

Once you have your keywords, it's time to incorporate them into your content. This is what's known as on-page SEO. There are a number of places where you'll want to include your keywords:

Title: Your title should be catchy, engaging, and include your primary keyword.

Headers: Headers help break up your content and make it easier to read. Try to include your keywords in at least a few of your headers.

Body: Naturally incorporate keywords throughout your content. But remember, write for humans, not search engines. Your content should still be engaging and easy to read.

URL: If possible, include your keyword in your URL. This helps search engines understand what your content is about.

Meta Description: This is the short snippet that appears under your title in search results. Make it enticing and include your keyword.

Image Alt Text: If you use images, don't forget to include your keyword in the image's alt text. This helps search engines understand what the image is about.

Off-Page SEO: Building Your Site's Reputation

On-page SEO is crucial, but it's just one piece of the puzzle. Off-page SEO refers to actions you take outside of your own website to impact your rankings within search engine results pages (SERPs). This primarily refers to backlinks, which are links from other websites to your content. Search engines view backlinks as a sign of credibility and authority, so the more quality backlinks you have, the better your content will rank.

SEO is a Marathon, Not a Sprint

Now, here's the thing: SEO takes time. It's not a one-and-done thing, and you won't see results overnight. It's a long-term strategy, but one that pays off immensely if you stick with it.

So there you have it, a crash course in SEO for affiliate marketing! Remember, the world of SEO is vast and constantly evolving, but by grasping these basic concepts, you're already well on your way. So go forth, optimize, and let the traffic roll in!

See, that wasn't too technical, was it? With a little bit of practice, you'll get the hang of SEO in no time, and you'll start to see the superpower that it really is in the world of affiliate marketing. Stay tuned for the next section where we will talk about strategies for continually creating content. It's going to be another exciting ride!

Let's continue our journey by diving into strategies for continually creating content. I know, it sounds like a marathon, right? But here's the deal – consistency is one of the most critical factors in your success as an affiliate marketer. Creating valuable content isn't just a one-time event; it's an ongoing process. Don't worry though, I'm here to guide you through this, and by the end of this section, you'll have a whole host of strategies under your belt to keep that content coming.

Why Is Consistent Content Important?

Before we jump into the strategies, let's talk a little about why this is so important. The first reason is all about SEO (search engine optimization). Search engines love fresh, new content. Every time you publish a new post, that's one more indexed page on your website, which boosts your visibility on search engine results.

The second reason is your audience. Consistent content keeps them engaged and coming back for more. Think about it. If you visited a blog that hadn't been updated in months, would you be likely to check back regularly? Probably not.

Now that we understand why we need to keep the content train chugging along, let's look at some strategies to help us do just that.

1. Content Planning

A content calendar can be your best friend here. This involves planning out your content for the coming weeks or even months. Consider any upcoming holidays, events, or product launches that might be relevant to your audience, and plan content around these. Not only does this help ensure you always have something in the pipeline, it can also take some of the stress out of content creation.

2. Mix Up Your Content Types

Different types of content can engage different segments of your audience, and also keep things interesting for you as a creator.

Blog posts, videos, podcasts, infographics, how-to guides – the possibilities are endless! Just make sure whatever you create provides value to your audience and fits with your overall brand and message..

3. Outsourcing

As your affiliate marketing efforts grow, you might find yourself struggling to keep up with the content demand. This is where outsourcing can be incredibly helpful. There are plenty of freelancers and content creation agencies out there who can produce high-quality content for you. Sites like Upwork or Fiverr can be great places to start looking.

4. User-Generated Content

User-generated content, or UGC, can be a fantastic way to both engage your audience and keep fresh content flowing. This could be anything from featuring customer testimonials or stories to holding contests where users submit their own content related to your niche. Not only does this provide you with free content, but it also makes your audience feel more connected and involved with your brand.

Don't be afraid to repurpose your old content. This could mean turning a blog post into a video or podcast episode, creating an infographic out of the data in a post, or even just updating an old post with new information.

Now, these are just a few strategies, but they should give you a good starting point. The key takeaway here is that creating consistent content is both important and manageable with the right strategies in place. Your content is the vehicle for your affiliate links, so it needs to be a priority in your affiliate marketing journey.

Remember, it's all about planning, being creative, and utilizing the resources available to you. You've got this! Stay tuned in as we dive into the next chapter - promoting your affiliate products.

Chapter 7: Promoting Your Affiliate Products

Alright, folks, it's time to dive into the really fun part – promoting your affiliate products. You've done all the legwork: you've understood the concept of affiliate marketing, set clear goals, built an online presence, and created fantastic content.

Now it's time to make your work visible and begin making that passive income!

Social Media Promotion

Now, folks, let's break down this beast called social media promotion. It might seem overwhelming at first, but trust me, once you get the hang of it, you're going to love the potential it has for promoting your affiliate products. Social media is an absolute powerhouse in today's digital world, with more than 3.6 billion people using it worldwide. Yep, you read that right! It's a sea full of potential customers, and you just need the right bait to reel them in.

Each social media platform has its own unique audience and vibe, so first things first, you need to understand which platforms align with your target audience and your niche. For example, if you're promoting affiliate products related to fashion, home decor, or food, you might find a more engaged audience on visually-driven platforms like Instagram or Pinterest. On the other hand, if you're promoting business or tech-related products, LinkedIn and Twitter could be your gold mines.

Remember, just because a platform has a massive number of users doesn't necessarily mean it's the right fit for you. Trying to be everywhere at once can lead to burnout, and honestly, your time could be better spent. So, pick a few platforms that align best with your goals, and focus on making your presence felt there.

Now, let's talk about the kind of content you should be sharing. It's crucial to maintain a good mix of promotional and non-promotional content. No one likes to follow someone who's constantly trying to sell them something, right? Instead, share valuable tips, industry news, behind-the-scenes looks, personal stories, user-generated content, and more. This way, you're providing value and building a relationship with your audience, making them more receptive when you do share your affiliate links.

Speaking of affiliate links, it's vital to be transparent about them. Most social media platforms require you to disclose if a link you're sharing could earn you money. A simple "#ad" or "#affiliate" is typically enough, but make sure you're familiar with the specific requirements of each platform. Honesty builds trust, and trust is what will get people to click your links and make a purchase.

Another key aspect of social media promotion is engagement. And no, I'm not just talking about the likes and comments on your posts. I'm talking about genuine interaction - responding to comments, asking your audience questions, getting involved in relevant conversations, and even following or engaging with other accounts in your niche. This not only helps increase the visibility of your posts (thanks to those handy-dandy algorithms) but also builds a sense of community around your brand.

And then there's the world of hashtags. These little symbols have the power to vastly increase the reach of your posts. Most platforms have a search feature for hashtags, which means that even people who don't follow you can discover your posts if they're looking at that hashtag. It's a good idea to use a combination of popular, moderately popular, and niche-specific hashtags to maximize your reach.

Last but not least, consider investing in social media ads. This can be particularly useful when you're just starting out and don't have a large following yet. Platforms like Facebook and Instagram offer relatively affordable advertising options that can help boost your visibility. You can target your ads based on things like age, location, interests, and more, ensuring they get in front of the right eyes.

Whew! That was quite a bit, wasn't it? Social media promotion is a vast and ever-changing landscape, but don't let that intimidate you. Start with these basics, learn as you go, and don't be afraid to experiment and see what works best for your unique audience and niche. And most importantly, have fun with it!

Email Marketing Strategies

Okay, let's chat about email marketing. I know, I know, it sounds a bit 'old school' in the age of social media, doesn't it? But, let me tell you, it's one of the most effective methods to promote your affiliate products. Don't believe me? Well, stats suggest that for every $1 you spend on email marketing, you can expect an average return of $42. That's a heck of a ROI! Let's dig into why it's so effective and how you can leverage it.

First things first, email is personal. When someone signs up to your email list, they're inviting you into their inbox, which is kind of a big deal. They're saying they want to hear from you, that they're interested in what you have to say, and that's a golden opportunity for affiliate marketers. It allows you to build a relationship with your audience, providing them with valuable content, and gradually introducing them to the affiliate products that you believe in.

So, how do you build an email list? One common method is through lead magnets - these are free resources that you offer your website visitors in exchange for their email addresses. It could be an eBook, a checklist, a discount code, a webinar, anything that offers value to your audience. If you make the lead magnet enticing enough, people will be willing to trade their email addresses for it.

Once you've got them on your list, it's all about nurturing that relationship. Regularly send them helpful, engaging content. This could be a weekly newsletter, blog post updates, tips and advice, industry news, or exclusive offers. The key here is consistency and quality. If you're consistently delivering value, your audience will start to look forward to your emails and will be more likely to engage with your affiliate links when you include them.

When it comes to promoting your affiliate products in your emails, subtlety is the name of the game. Remember, no one likes being sold to. Instead of just blasting out promotional emails, try to weave your affiliate links into your content naturally. For example, if you're sending an email with tips on how to get a good night's sleep, and you're an affiliate for a sleep aid product, include a link to that product within your tips. Make it feel like a natural part of the conversation, not an ad.

Now, if you're thinking, "But how do I keep track of all these emails?!" don't worry, there are plenty of email marketing tools out there to help you manage your list, automate your emails, and even analyze your results. Some popular ones are Mailchimp, ConvertKit, and AWeber. Do some research, see which one fits your needs and budget, and give it a go!

Another critical thing to remember is to always be compliant with email marketing laws. The CAN-SPAM Act, for example, requires that you clearly identify yourself, include your physical address, and provide a way for recipients to opt-out of your emails. So make sure you familiarize yourself with these laws to stay on the right side of things.

I won't lie, building and maintaining an email list takes work. But the potential benefits for your affiliate marketing business are huge. It's a direct line of communication with your audience, allowing you to build trust, deliver value, and promote your affiliate products in a personal, non-pushy way. So why not give it a shot?

Paid Advertising: Pros, Cons, and Best Practices

Now that we've talked about using email and social media to promote your affiliate products, let's delve into the exciting world of paid advertising. Yep, this is the part where we put our money where our mouth is!

First, let's understand what paid advertising is. Simply put, paid advertising is a marketing strategy that involves paying for ad space to promote a product or service. This could be anything from a banner ad on a website to a sponsored post on Instagram or even a YouTube ad. In affiliate marketing, paid advertising can be a great way to get your affiliate links in front of a wider audience.

The Pros of Paid Advertising

The benefits of paid advertising are pretty evident. It allows you to reach a large number of people quickly, including those who might not be in your immediate network. It also provides an opportunity to target your ads based on specific demographics like age, location, interests, and behavior. This means you can focus your efforts on people who are most likely to be interested in your affiliate products.

Another advantage of paid advertising is that it's scalable. You can start with a small budget, test out your ads, and once you find what works, you can increase your budget and reach even more people. It's also measurable, meaning you can track the performance of your ads in real-time and tweak them as needed for better results.

The Cons of Paid Advertising

However, like anything in life, paid advertising also comes with its challenges. First, it can be expensive. If you're just starting out with limited funds, it might be challenging to invest in paid advertising.

Another potential drawback is competition. Many sectors are highly competitive when it comes to paid advertising, which can drive up the costs. If you're in such a sector, you'll have to find a way to make your ads stand out.

Best Practices for Paid Advertising in Affiliate Marketing

So, how do you navigate this world of paid advertising in affiliate marketing? Here are a few best practices to guide you.

Know Your Audience: Before you start any paid advertising campaign, it's crucial to know who your audience is. What are their interests? What problems are they trying to solve? Knowing your audience will help you create ads that resonate with them.

Choose the Right Platforms: Not all advertising platforms will be a good fit for your affiliate products. Do your research and choose platforms that your target audience uses and engages with.

Test, Test, Test: This is where the magic happens. Test different ads, headlines, images, and call-to-actions to see what resonates with your audience. It's all about finding what works and iterating on that.

Track Your Performance: Use analytics to measure the success of your ads. Are they driving traffic? Are they leading to conversions? Use this information to refine your ads and make them more effective.

Mind the Rules: Different platforms have different rules regarding affiliate links, so make sure to familiarize yourself with these before launching your campaigns.

Be Patient: It might take some time to see results from your paid advertising efforts. Don't get discouraged if you don't see immediate results. Keep refining your approach and stay patient.

While paid advertising does come with a cost, when done right, it can be a powerful tool in your affiliate marketing arsenal. So, if you're ready to expand your reach and take your affiliate marketing to the next level, it might be worth exploring this option. Just remember to start small, test your ads, and keep refining your approach based on your results. And most importantly, have fun with it!

Collaborations and Partnerships

Finally, let's venture into the realm of collaborations and partnerships. This is where you get to work directly with other individuals or businesses to amplify your reach and, ultimately, your affiliate marketing success.

"Collaborations" and "partnerships" might sound like big, fancy words that are reserved only for established brands or influencers, but that couldn't be further from the truth. In fact, in the world of affiliate marketing, collaborations and partnerships are not only attainable for beginners, but they are also incredibly effective tools for growth.

So, what exactly are collaborations and partnerships, and how do they fit into your affiliate marketing strategy?

Understanding Collaborations and Partnerships

Collaborations often involve working together with other content creators or influencers to create or promote content. You could do a guest blog post, participate in a podcast, or co-host a webinar, just to name a few examples.

Partnerships, on the other hand, tend to be more long-term and structured. They often involve forming an ongoing relationship with a company or brand, where both parties benefit from promoting each other's products or services.

Why Collaborations and Partnerships Matter

Collaborations and partnerships can open up an entirely new audience for your affiliate marketing efforts. By collaborating with someone who has a following, you can gain access to their audience and expose your affiliate products to a wider group of potential customers.

Moreover, collaborations and partnerships can lend credibility to your affiliate marketing business. If you collaborate with a respected individual or brand, their audience is more likely to trust your recommendations. This trust can translate into higher click-through rates and more conversions on your affiliate links.

Finding the Right Collaborations and Partnerships

Now, the question is: how do you find the right collaborations and partnerships? Here are a few tips to get you started:

Look for a Good Fit: Start by looking for individuals or businesses that complement your affiliate niche. Their audience should be similar to yours, so there's a higher chance they will be interested in your affiliate products.

Do Your Homework: Research potential collaborators or partners thoroughly. Check out their online presence, what their audience engagement is like, and whether their brand values align with yours.

Reach Out: Don't be shy about reaching out to potential collaborators or partners. Remember, it's a two-way street, and they also stand to benefit from working with you.

Making Collaborations and Partnerships Work

Once you've established a collaboration or partnership, it's crucial to nurture that relationship. Be proactive, responsive, and open to feedback. Also, make sure the collaboration or partnership is mutually beneficial. It shouldn't be just about what you can gain from the relationship but also about how you can contribute to their success.

Navigating Challenges

Of course, collaborations and partnerships can also come with their own set of challenges. You might find that you don't see eye to eye on every decision or that it takes more time than you anticipated. But remember, every challenge is also an opportunity for growth. Be patient, stay open to learning, and remember, you're not alone in this journey.

To wrap up, collaborations and partnerships can be a powerful way to enhance your affiliate marketing efforts. By combining your strengths with those of another individual or brand, you can reach more people, build trust, and ultimately boost your affiliate earnings. So go on, step out of your comfort zone, and start exploring the opportunities that collaborations and partnerships can offer!

Chapter 8: Tracking and Optimizing Your Performance

In the world of affiliate marketing, you don't just "set it and forget it." One of the keys to successful affiliate marketing is continually monitoring, tracking, and optimizing your performance. In this chapter, we'll dive deep into how to do that effectively.

Importance of Analytics

Okay, friends, let's think of affiliate marketing as an intricate dance routine, each step carefully choreographed to lead to the next. Now imagine executing this dance in complete darkness. Not so easy, right? Well, operating your affiliate marketing business without the guidance of analytics is much like dancing in the dark. You might be moving, but you don't exactly know where you're going or if you're stepping on someone's toes. Analytics lights up the dance floor, helping you see where to step next.

Analytics in affiliate marketing is essentially about understanding your data – clicks, conversion rates, visitor demographics, buyer behavior, and so much more. It involves taking these raw numbers and turning them into actionable insights. It's the compass that guides your decision-making process, leading you towards more profitable campaigns.

To put it simply, analytics equals knowledge, and as we all know, knowledge is power. When you know who your audience is, where they're coming from, what they're interested in, and what triggers them to make a purchase, you're in a much better position to serve them effectively.

Let's break down some specific areas where analytics prove their worth:

1. Understanding Your Audience: It's one thing to assume who your target audience is, but it's another thing to know for sure. With analytics, you can know the age, gender, location, and even the devices your audience uses. This way, you can tailor your content and promotions to suit their specific needs and preferences.

2. Evaluating Your Performance: Here's the brutal truth: not all your efforts will work. Some blog posts will flop, some promotions will go unnoticed, and some affiliate products won't sell. That's just part of the game. But with analytics, you don't have to rely on guesswork to identify what's working and what's not. You have concrete data to evaluate your performance.

3. Optimizing Your Strategies: Armed with data from analytics, you can optimize your strategies for better results. For instance, if you find that most of your website visitors are coming from Facebook, it might make sense to intensify your Facebook marketing efforts. If a particular type of blog post format is leading to more conversions, you can create more of such posts.

4. Setting and Tracking Your Goals: Remember those SMART goals we talked about earlier? Well, analytics is the key to setting realistic goals and tracking your progress towards them. You can set goals based on your past performance and use analytics to monitor your progress regularly.

5. Predicting Future Trends: Now, this is where it gets really exciting. With enough data, you can start to notice trends and patterns in your affiliate marketing performance. This can help you predict future trends, giving you a head start in adjusting your strategies.

6. Maximizing Your Earnings: Ultimately, all this tracking and optimizing leads to one thing - increased earnings. By understanding what drives clicks and conversions, you can focus your efforts on the most profitable strategies, leading to better ROI.

The bottom line is this: if you're serious about succeeding in affiliate marketing, you can't afford to ignore analytics. It's not just about having a bunch of numbers and charts. It's about gaining deep insights into your business, your audience, and your performance. With these insights, you can make informed decisions, optimize your strategies, and continually grow your affiliate marketing earnings. Analytics, my friends, is the secret sauce to your affiliate marketing success.

Using Tools for Tracking Performance

Now that we've established how important analytics is, let's move on to another essential topic: the tools that help you track your performance.

Just like a carpenter wouldn't get far without their trusty toolbox, affiliate marketers also need a set of tools to keep their business running smoothly.

But with so many tracking tools available in the digital market, how do you choose which ones are right for your affiliate marketing business? I've got you covered. We'll delve into the different types of tools you may need, what they can do for you, and how to go about selecting the right ones.

1. Affiliate Network Tracking Tools: Most affiliate networks provide their own in-house tracking tools. These typically provide a range of data, including clicks, conversions, commission earned, and sometimes even customer demographics. While these tools can vary in their level of detail and complexity, they offer an excellent starting point for your tracking needs.

2. Website Analytics Tools: When it comes to understanding how users interact with your website, tools like Google Analytics can be indispensable. Google Analytics allows you to see where your traffic is coming from, which pages are the most popular, how long users are staying on your site, and a whole lot more.

3. Social Media Analytics Tools: If you're using social media as part of your promotional strategy, you'll need tools to track your performance. Platforms like Facebook, Instagram, Twitter, and LinkedIn all have built-in analytics features. These can help you track your follower count, post engagement, and even the best times to post.

4. Email Marketing Analytics Tools: For those who utilize email marketing in their strategy, email service providers like MailChimp or ConvertKit provide comprehensive analytics features. You can track open rates, click-through rates, and even see which part of your email got the most engagement.

5. SEO Tools: SEO, or search engine optimization, is an essential part of affiliate marketing. SEO tools like SEMrush and Moz can provide detailed insights into your website's search performance, identify opportunities for improvement, and help you keep an eye on the competition.

6. A/B Testing Tools: These tools help you test different versions of your web pages, emails, or ads to see which one performs better. Tools like Optimizely or VWO provide easy-to-use platforms for running these tests and analyzing the results.

Now that you're familiar with the types of tools available, how do you go about choosing the right ones for your business? Well, there are a few things to consider:

a. Your Goals: Different tools serve different purposes. Identify your specific goals first, whether it's to increase website traffic, improve email engagement, or boost conversion rates, then choose the tool that aligns with those goals.

b. Your Budget: Some of these tools are free, some offer free versions with limited features, and others require a monthly or annual subscription. Be clear about how much you're willing and able to spend on these tools.

c. Ease of Use: Some tools are easier to use than others. If you're not particularly tech-savvy, look for tools that are user-friendly and offer good customer support.

d. Integration: Ideally, the tools you choose should integrate well with each other for streamlined operations. For instance, your email marketing tool should easily integrate with your website platform.

Remember, these tools are there to make your life easier, not more complicated. Start with the basics and then gradually add more tools as your affiliate marketing business grows and your needs become more complex. Tracking your performance is not a one-size-fits-all process, but with the right tools, it becomes a lot more manageable.

Interpreting Data and Making Improvements

So, you've started collecting data with your shiny new tools. That's fantastic, you're on the right track. But, now comes the question, what do you do with all these numbers and statistics? They might seem like random digits at first, but these numbers actually tell a story — a story about your performance, your audience, and your marketing efforts. It's crucial to understand this story to continually make improvements. But how do you decipher it? Let's take it one step at a time.

1. Understand Your Metrics: This is where it all starts. You need to understand what each metric means and why it's important. For instance, knowing the difference between 'clicks' and 'conversions', or 'bounce rate' and 'exit rate', can be crucial. The definitions might seem similar, but in the world of affiliate marketing, they hold very different implications. So take some time, research, and familiarize yourself with these metrics.

2. Identify Your KPIs: KPI stands for Key Performance Indicator. As the name suggests, these are the metrics that matter the most to you and your business goals. They can vary depending on your strategy and what you're trying to achieve. For example, if your goal is to increase brand awareness, then metrics like social shares, comments, or follower count might be your KPIs. On the other hand, if you aim to increase sales, then your conversion rate would be a more relevant KPI.

3. Analyze the Trends: Now that you're familiar with your metrics and KPIs, it's time to analyze. Look for trends and patterns. Are your website visits increasing month by month? Are users staying longer on your site? Are your email open rates going up or down? These trends can tell you a lot about what's working and what's not in your marketing efforts.

4. Connect the Dots: This is where you start linking cause and effect. For instance, if you notice a spike in website visits the day after you send out your monthly newsletter, there's likely a connection. Similarly, if you observe a decline in social media engagement when you post less frequently, that's valuable information too.

5. Dive Deeper: If you notice any anomalies or significant changes, don't be afraid to dig a little deeper. If your conversion rate has suddenly dropped, try to figure out why. Did you make changes to your website? Has there been a shift in your audience's behavior? Remember, the devil often lies in the details.

6. Make Data-Driven Decisions: Use your findings to make informed decisions. If your data suggests that your audience is most active on social media in the evenings, consider scheduling your posts around that time. If a particular type of blog post is driving a lot of traffic, produce more similar content. Your data is your guide here.

7. Keep Testing and Tweaking: Lastly, remember that interpreting data and making improvements is not a one-off process. It's continuous. Trends change, algorithms evolve, audiences shift. Keep testing new strategies, tweaking based on results, and evolving along with the market.

Interpreting data might seem overwhelming at first, but it's really like reading a book once you know the language. It's about being curious, asking questions, and not being afraid to dig deeper. And with time, it becomes an integral part of your business, helping you navigate the complex world of affiliate marketing with confidence and informed decisions.

Keep in mind that numbers tell a story, but they don't tell the whole story. Be open to qualitative insights as well. Listen to your audience, be attentive to their feedback and preferences, because while data can guide you to a certain extent, the human element is just as crucial, if not more. And above all, remember that improvement is a journey, not a destination. The affiliate marketing landscape is ever-changing, and success lies in adapting and growing with it. Keep learning, keep iterating, and keep moving forward.

A/B Testing

Alright, now let's talk about something that's going to be your new best friend in affiliate marketing: A/B testing. If you're unfamiliar with the term, no worries at all. This is why we're here together, right?

1. What is A/B Testing?: At its most basic, A/B testing is like a science experiment for your marketing strategy. You have two versions of something (version A and version B, hence the name), and you're testing to see which one performs better. This 'something' could be an email subject line, a call-to-action on your website, a product image, or just about anything else you can think of. The idea is to change one variable at a time so you can attribute any difference in results to that variable.

2. Why is A/B Testing Important?: This is where things start to get exciting. A/B testing is important because it allows you to make data-driven decisions about changes to your marketing strategy. Instead of making a change and hoping for the best, A/B testing lets you make informed decisions based on actual data. Think of it as a compass guiding your journey through the sometimes-confusing world of affiliate marketing.

3. Planning Your A/B Tests: Okay, so now that you know what A/B testing is and why it's important, how do you go about setting up an A/B test? Well, the first step is to identify what you want to test. This could be anything from the color of a button on your website to the wording of a call to action in an email. Once you've identified what you want to test, you need to create your two versions (version A and version B). Remember, only change one variable between the versions, otherwise, you won't know what caused any differences in performance.

4. Implementing Your A/B Tests: After you've created your two versions, the next step is to implement your test. You'll show version A to one half of your audience, and version B to the other half. There are many tools available that can help with this process, from website plugins to email marketing software.

5. Analyzing Your A/B Test Results: Once your A/B test is complete, it's time to analyze the results. Which version performed better? Why do you think that is? This is where your detective skills come in handy. Your findings will give you insights that can inform your future marketing efforts.

6. Rinse and Repeat: A/B testing isn't a one-time thing. It's a continuous process of testing, learning, and improving. After your first A/B test, identify a new variable to test, and start the process over again.

A/B testing might seem like a lot of work, but it's worth it. Small changes can have a big impact on your affiliate marketing performance. It's all about refining and optimizing, and A/B testing is a key tool in your optimization toolkit.

Like most things in affiliate marketing (and life!), A/B testing is a learning process. Your first few tests might not yield dramatic results, and that's okay. Don't be discouraged. Remember, every test gives you data, and data is a powerful thing. So keep testing, keep learning, and keep improving. Before you know it, you'll be an A/B testing pro, making data-driven decisions and continually improving your affiliate marketing performance. And along the way, you'll become more and more comfortable with interpreting your data and making informed decisions - decisions that bring you closer to your goals. Because at the end of the day, that's what it's all about: reaching your goals and becoming your own affiliate marketing hero.

Chapter 9: Navigating Affiliate Marketing Laws and Ethics

We're going to shift gears a bit now and talk about something really important, yet often overlooked by beginners: the legal and ethical aspects of affiliate marketing. It's not the most glamorous or exciting part of this journey, but trust me, it's essential knowledge. We don't want any unpleasant surprises down the road, do we?

Understanding the Legal Aspects

Alright, let's dig a bit deeper into the legal aspects. Like I said before, this isn't the most thrilling topic, but trust me, it's crucial.

When you think about it, this legal stuff is really all about protecting yourself and your affiliate marketing business.

Let's start by making one thing clear: affiliate marketing, just like any other business, operates within a legal framework. Now, this might sound a bit daunting, especially if you're just starting out and are eager to get into the fun stuff, like choosing products and promoting them. But trust me, understanding the legalities involved in affiliate marketing is going to help you in the long run.

Think of it as building a sturdy foundation for your affiliate marketing mansion. You wouldn't want to build a grand mansion on shaky ground, would you? The same goes for your affiliate marketing business - you want to build it on a solid legal foundation to avoid any hiccups or disasters down the line.

1. Contracts

When you sign up to join an affiliate program, you'll often need to agree to a contract or terms of service. These documents can seem long and complicated, especially with all the legal jargon. However, it's essential that you read these thoroughly.

These contracts outline your rights and responsibilities as an affiliate. They'll explain what you can and can't do when promoting the merchant's products, and how and when you'll get paid. Some contracts might also have clauses about where you can advertise, how you can use the merchant's branding, and what happens if you break the terms of the agreement.

So, before you click 'I Agree', make sure you actually understand what you're agreeing to. If there's anything you're unsure about, it's always a good idea to seek legal advice.

2. Privacy Laws

Another important legal aspect to be aware of is privacy laws. If you're collecting any sort of personal data from your site visitors, whether it's through a contact form, email sign-up form, or even just through cookies tracking visitor behavior on your site, you need to be aware of the relevant privacy laws.

In the United States, this is governed by laws like the Children's Online Privacy Protection Act (COPPA) and the California Consumer Privacy Act (CCPA). In the European Union, it's the General Data Protection Regulation (GDPR).

These laws have different requirements, but in general, they require websites to have a clear and accessible privacy policy that explains what data is collected and how it's used.

Complying with privacy laws isn't just about avoiding legal trouble. It's also about building trust with your site visitors. When people know their data is being handled responsibly, they're more likely to feel comfortable interacting with your site and taking actions like clicking on affiliate links or signing up for a newsletter.

3. Advertising Laws

Finally, we have advertising laws. As an affiliate marketer, you're essentially advertising products on behalf of merchants. This means you need to be aware of the laws around what you can and can't say in these advertisements.

In many countries, it's against the law to make false or misleading claims about products. This includes exaggerating the benefits of a product, hiding important information about it, or making unsupported claims. Laws like the U.S. Federal Trade Commission's (FTC) Truth in Advertising rules set out clear guidelines on this.

As an affiliate marketer, it's your responsibility to ensure that all the product descriptions, reviews, and recommendations on your site comply with these rules. This is part of being a responsible and ethical affiliate marketer.

In conclusion, navigating the legal aspects of affiliate marketing might seem overwhelming at first, but it's a vital part of running your business. By understanding the basics of contract law, privacy laws, and advertising laws, you're setting yourself up for long-term success. In our next section, we'll look at ethical guidelines and best practices to ensure your affiliate marketing is not just legally compliant, but also morally sound.

Ethical Guidelines and Best Practices

Alright, moving on to something a little less dry but equally important: the ethics of affiliate marketing. After all, success isn't just about making money – it's about how you make it.

When you engage in affiliate marketing, it's easy to get caught up in the allure of earning passive income and overlook the ethical considerations that come into play. But hold on a minute! The truth is, how you conduct your affiliate marketing business matters just as much as what you earn from it.

Here's the thing. Ethical affiliate marketing isn't just about following the law – it's about building trust, maintaining transparency, and promoting products responsibly. Let's break that down.

1. Building Trust

First things first, building trust is crucial in affiliate marketing. Your readers come to your website or social media page for information they can rely on. Whether they're looking for product reviews, advice, or resources, they want to know that they can trust your recommendations.

Here's where ethics come into play. It's not just about promoting products that will earn you the most commission. It's about recommending products that you believe in and that you think will truly benefit your audience. This means doing your research, testing products where possible, and giving honest reviews.

If your audience trusts you, they're more likely to click on your affiliate links and make purchases. And trust me, once you lose that trust, it's tough to regain.

2. Maintaining Transparency

Transparency is another biggie. Being upfront about your affiliate relationships is not just good practice – it's also the law in many countries. When you use affiliate links, you should disclose this to your audience.

This can be as simple as including a statement at the top of your posts or on your site that says you may earn a commission for purchases made through your links. Many affiliate marketers also include a more detailed disclosure in their site's footer or about page.

Again, this is about building trust. When you're upfront with your readers, they're more likely to respect your honesty and continue to support you.

3. Promoting Products Responsibly

Lastly, let's talk about promoting products responsibly. As an affiliate marketer, you have a responsibility to ensure that the products you're promoting are reliable, safe, and worth the price.

This means not promoting products you haven't researched, or products from shady companies that might scam your readers. It also means not pushing people to buy products they don't need or can't afford.

Always put your audience's needs and best interests first. It's not just about making a sale, it's about adding value to your readers' lives.

Here's the takeaway: Ethical affiliate marketing is a win-win. It helps you build a trustworthy brand, create a loyal audience, and sustain a long-term business. In the next section, we'll delve into the specific disclosure requirements to keep your affiliate marketing transparent and above-board. Remember, it's not just about doing well - it's about doing good. As an ethical affiliate marketer, you're in a position to make a real difference in people's lives. So, let's get out there and do it right!

Disclosure Requirements

In affiliate marketing, transparency isn't just a best practice, it's a legal requirement. Yep, you heard it right! In many parts of the world, including the United States, you're legally obliged to disclose your affiliate relationships to your audience. Here's what you need to know.

1. Why Disclosure Is Required

The main reason for these disclosure requirements is to protect consumers. It's all about ensuring people have the information they need to make informed decisions. If your audience knows you're getting paid when they click on a link and make a purchase, they can take this into consideration when deciding whether to trust your recommendation.

Plus, let's be real, wouldn't you want to know if someone was getting a cut from a product they're recommending?

2. Where and When to Disclose

The Federal Trade Commission (FTC) in the United States has guidelines on how and when you need to disclose your affiliate relationships. The key is to make sure your disclosure is clear and conspicuous. This means it should be easy to see and understand.

A quick note at the end of a blog post probably won't cut it. It's better to put your disclosure near the affiliate links – ideally, before them. It should also stand out, so don't just bury it in a bunch of other text or hide it in the footer of your site.

One common approach is to put a disclosure at the top of blog posts that contain affiliate links. You can also include a more detailed disclosure on a separate page of your site and link to it from your posts.

As for when to disclose, the rule is pretty straightforward: you need to disclose whenever you use affiliate links. This includes not just blog posts, but also social media posts, emails, YouTube videos – anywhere and everywhere you use affiliate links.

3. What to Say in Your Disclosure

There's no one-size-fits-all script for affiliate disclosures, but there are a few key points you should cover. First, make it clear that you may earn a commission for purchases made through your links. Second, reassure your audience that this doesn't affect the price they pay.

It's also a good idea to note that you only recommend products you believe in. This isn't legally required, but it can help build trust with your audience.

Here's an example of a simple disclosure: "This post contains affiliate links. This means I may earn a commission, at no extra cost to you, if you make a purchase through these links. I only recommend products I believe in."

4. Staying Up-to-Date

Laws and guidelines can change, so it's important to stay up-to-date. The FTC periodically releases updates to its guidelines, so keep an eye on their website. If you're outside the United States, check the laws in your country.

The takeaway? Yes, disclosure requirements can seem like a chore, but they're important. They help protect consumers, they help build trust with your audience, and they keep you on the right side of the law. So embrace them, don't fear them. Be proud to disclose your affiliate relationships – it shows that you're committed to transparency and honesty.

Alright, with the legalities out of the way, we can get back to the fun stuff. In the next chapters, we'll cover how to grow your affiliate marketing business.

Chapter 10: Growing Your Affiliate Marketing Business

Building Relationships with Merchants

Let's start by diving into the realm of relationships in the affiliate marketing world. As we progress on this journey of growth, it's crucial to consider the relationships that lay the groundwork for our success, particularly those with our merchants. So, let's break it down together.

1. The Significance of Relationships in Affiliate Marketing

Alright, so why should you bother with building relationships in the first place? Well, in the world of affiliate marketing, establishing solid relationships with your merchants is not just about good manners—it's a business strategy that can pay off in spades.

Let's think about it this way. A strong, positive relationship with your merchant means you have a reliable partner who values your input, and vice versa. It's like being part of a team where each player has a clear understanding of their role, and they work towards the same goals, appreciating the input and contributions of others.

By nurturing a positive relationship, you can enjoy various benefits, such as exclusive deals and higher commissions, which can drastically improve your earnings. Moreover, it can lead to early access to new products or services, giving you a competitive edge in your niche.

But beyond the monetary incentives, having a trustworthy relationship creates an environment of mutual respect. This sort of relationship opens up opportunities for learning, feedback, and growth that can enhance your career in ways you never anticipated.

2. The Art of Building Relationships with Merchants

Building relationships with merchants is not some sort of cryptic science. It's an art—a delicate dance of communication, understanding, respect, and mutual benefit. And like any good dance, it requires practice, patience, and a willingness to learn.

At the heart of it all is communication. A healthy relationship is built on understanding each other's goals, expectations, and constraints. Regular, open, and honest communication helps avoid misunderstandings and fosters mutual trust. And trust me, trust goes a long way in any relationship.

Remember, though, this isn't a quick process—it takes time. You've got to be consistent, respectful, and professional. Show interest in your merchant's business and products. Be proactive in learning about their company and industry. Your curiosity and commitment can demonstrate that you're not just interested in a quick profit, but in contributing to their success, too.

3. Nurturing and Maintaining Relationships

Okay, so you've built a relationship. Congratulations! But remember, maintaining this relationship is just as crucial as building it. It's like tending to a garden—you've planted the seeds, now you need to water and nourish them.

You want to keep the lines of communication open and engage with your merchant regularly. You don't need to be best buddies, but sharing your successes, seeking advice, and giving feedback keeps you on their radar and shows that you're serious about your role as an affiliate.

But here's the catch. You have to deal with the bad times as well as the good ones. If there's a problem or an issue, tackle it head-on. Be proactive in addressing any concerns and work towards finding a solution. This shows your merchant that you're dependable and committed, even when things get tough.

And let's not forget, relationships are a two-way street. Just as you expect your merchant to respect and value you, you must also offer them the same courtesy. Think about ways to add value to their business, whether that's through driving more sales, providing customer feedback, or promoting their brand.

So, there you have it. The ins and outs of building and maintaining relationships with your merchants. And remember, all this effort isn't just for the sake of politeness—it's a strategic move that can fuel your business growth.

Diversifying Your Affiliate Portfolio

Alright, so let's dive into the concept of diversifying your affiliate portfolio. Sounds a bit finance-y, right? But don't worry, we're going to break it down into bite-sized pieces that are easier to digest.

1. Understanding the Concept of Diversification in Affiliate Marketing

In the world of affiliate marketing, diversification is all about not putting all your eggs in one basket. The idea is to promote products from various merchants across different niches to spread your income sources.

It's like investing in the stock market—you wouldn't just buy stocks from one company, right? You'd spread your investments across different companies and sectors to reduce your risk. The same concept applies to affiliate marketing. Diversifying your affiliate portfolio helps you minimize risks and increase your earning potential.

2. Why Diversification is Important

So, why should you care about diversification? Let's imagine a scenario. Say you've partnered with a single merchant and they suddenly decide to shut down their affiliate program or, worse, their entire business. Boom, there goes your income stream.

But let's say you have a diversified portfolio. You've partnered with several merchants across different niches. Now, if one of them closes their affiliate program or business, it's a bummer, sure, but it won't be a total catastrophe. You still have other income sources to rely on.

And there's another benefit of diversification—tapping into multiple customer segments. By promoting products in various niches, you can reach a wider audience, boosting your potential earnings.

3. How to Diversify Your Affiliate Portfolio

Okay, so now we know what diversification is and why it's essential. But how do we go about it? Here's the thing—it's not as complicated as it might seem.

Start by examining your current affiliate partnerships. Are they all in the same niche? Do they all cater to the same customer segment? If so, it's time to explore new territories. Look for merchants in different niches that align with your content and audience. Remember, relevance is key. Promoting irrelevant products will only confuse your audience and could hurt your credibility.

While venturing into new niches, it's also a good idea to diversify the types of products you promote. For instance, you could mix physical products with digital ones like eBooks, online courses, or software.

Remember, diversification doesn't mean you should go on an affiliate program signing spree. Quality should always come before quantity. It's better to have a few high-quality, profitable partnerships than a bunch of low-performing ones. So do your research, pick your partners carefully, and always keep your audience's needs in mind.

4. Maintaining a Diversified Portfolio

Great, you've diversified your portfolio. But guess what? This isn't a set-it-and-forget-it type of thing. You need to actively maintain and tweak your portfolio to keep it balanced and profitable.

Keep a close eye on your performance metrics for each affiliate program. This will help you identify which partnerships are performing well and which ones are lagging behind. Don't be afraid to cut ties with low-performing programs and replace them with potentially more profitable ones.

Also, stay on top of market trends. Consumer needs and preferences can change, and new products or niches may emerge. Regularly review your portfolio to ensure it aligns with current trends and your audience's evolving needs.

Diversifying your affiliate portfolio is an effective strategy for reducing risks and boosting your income potential. It's a bit like a balancing act—it requires constant monitoring and adjustments. But with patience and diligence, you can create a diversified portfolio that ensures a steady and sustainable income stream.

Strategies for Scaling Your Business

Alright, now that you're getting the hang of this affiliate marketing thing and you have a diversified portfolio of affiliate partnerships, it's time to talk about growth. Scaling your business means increasing your income without significantly increasing your workload. So let's chat about some strategies to scale your affiliate marketing business.

1. Optimize Your Existing Content

The first thing you might want to consider is optimizing your existing content. Your old blog posts or YouTube videos could be a goldmine waiting to be discovered. Look through your older content and see if there are opportunities to include affiliate links where you haven't before. Also, update your content to ensure it remains relevant and continues to drive traffic.

2. Increase Your Traffic

More traffic generally leads to more conversions, so consider ways to increase the number of visitors to your website or viewers of your videos. There are many ways to do this, from improving your SEO to stepping up your social media game or even running paid ad campaigns. Just remember to target your marketing efforts to the right audience—those who are likely to be interested in the products you're promoting.

3. Leverage Email Marketing

Your email list is a potent tool for scaling your business. It gives you a direct line of communication with people who have expressed interest in your content. If you haven't started building an email list, now is the time. If you have one, consider ways to optimize your email marketing strategy.

Personalize your emails, segment your list, provide valuable content, and strategically include your affiliate links. An optimized email marketing strategy can significantly boost your conversion rates.

4. Try New Marketing Strategies

Don't be afraid to test new marketing strategies. The digital marketing landscape is constantly evolving, with new trends and techniques popping up all the time. You might discover a new strategy that significantly increases your conversions.

For instance, influencer marketing has become a big thing. Collaborating with influencers in your niche could give you access to a larger audience. Or you might try creating webinars or podcasts, if you haven't already. Always be open to trying new things and experimenting.

5. Automate Where You Can

Scaling your business will often involve doing more of what works, but you don't want to burn out by taking on too much work. This is where automation comes in.

Many aspects of affiliate marketing can be automated, freeing up your time for other things. From social media posting to email marketing, look for ways you can automate tasks without sacrificing quality or personalization.

6. Outsourcing Tasks

Similar to automation, outsourcing can also help you scale your business without getting overwhelmed. You might hire a virtual assistant to manage your social media accounts or a writer to help create content. Just remember to maintain quality control and ensure that everything aligns with your brand and voice.

7. Expand Your Product Range

Finally, consider expanding your product range. This could mean promoting more products within your existing niches, or it could mean branching out into new niches. Just remember the importance of relevance—only promote products that are valuable and relevant to your audience.

Scaling your affiliate marketing business is about working smarter, not harder. By optimizing your existing content, driving more traffic, leveraging your email list, trying new strategies, automating tasks, outsourcing, and expanding your product range, you can increase your income without increasing your workload exponentially. Now, that's smart business!

Chapter 11: Case Studies of Successful Affiliate Marketers

It's east to get overwhelmed as you read all about this stuff, but remember, you've come a long way already! Now let's take a look at some real-life examples of successful affiliate marketers who have transformed their lives and created profitable online businesses. These case studies provide valuable insights, tips, and inspiration that can help you on your affiliate marketing journey. Remember, if any of these people could make it - you can too!

Case Study 1: Pat Flynn

Pat Flynn, the founder of Smart Passive Income, is a prime example of affiliate marketing success. A former architect, Flynn found himself jobless during the 2008 economic crisis. Determined to create a more secure future, he ventured into online business and discovered affiliate marketing.

Flynn's approach to affiliate marketing is based on transparency, authenticity, and providing immense value to his audience. His platform, Smart Passive Income, is loaded with resources that help people create their own passive income streams. He shares in-depth tutorials, podcasts, blog posts, and even his own income reports.

These income reports are a cornerstone of his brand, providing tangible proof of his success while also maintaining transparency with his audience. Flynn consistently promotes products he has personally used and believes in, establishing trust with his audience and making him a go-to source for recommendations.

Case Study 2: Michelle Schroeder-Gardner

The creator of Making Sense of Cents, Michelle Schroeder-Gardner, transformed her passion for personal finance into a thriving online business. She started her blog to document her journey of paying off student loan debt and soon began sharing tips on saving money, budgeting, and generating income.

Schroeder-Gardner discovered affiliate marketing and recognized its potential to generate significant income. By consistently delivering high-quality, relevant content, and carefully selecting products that align with her audience's interests, she's built a loyal following. Her honesty about her own financial journey and her dedication to helping others manage their finances have been key to her success.

Case Study 3: Matthew Woodward

Matthew Woodward is a renowned internet marketer whose blog is a treasure trove of tips, tutorials, and case studies on SEO, affiliate marketing, and digital marketing strategies. He's built a successful business by sharing his expertise and dedication to helping others succeed online.

Woodward leverages his in-depth knowledge of SEO to drive organic traffic to his blog. He's well-known for his detailed case studies, where he takes readers step-by-step through different marketing strategies. By providing massive value and actionable content, Woodward has built a strong reputation and a loyal following in the digital marketing community.

Case Study 4: John Chow

John Chow, a prominent blogger and entrepreneur, stands out for his success in the product niche affiliate marketing. On his blog, John Chow dot Com, he shares tips and strategies for making money online.

Chow's expertise lies in promoting various products and services that align with his niche. His comprehensive reviews and personal experiences with the products he promotes add credibility to his recommendations and build trust with his audience.

Chow's approach to affiliate marketing, coupled with his engaging writing style, has helped him generate substantial income and establish a solid online presence.

These successful affiliate marketers started just like you, with a desire to create an income online and the determination to make it happen. Their journeys illustrate the potential of affiliate marketing and provide inspiration and practical strategies that you can apply to your own affiliate marketing business. Whether it's Pat Flynn's transparency, Michelle Schroeder-Gardner's passion, Matthew Woodward's in-depth knowledge, or John Chow's product expertise, there's a wealth of wisdom to glean from these successful affiliate marketers.

Conclusion: Your Journey from Zero to Passive Income Hero

We've covered a lot of ground together. From understanding the mechanics of affiliate marketing to studying successful case studies, you've taken a comprehensive tour of the affiliate marketing landscape. Let's recap our journey and look ahead to the next steps in your path to becoming a passive income hero.

Recap of the Affiliate Marketing Journey

Whew! We've been on quite a journey, haven't we? I'm excited to have been a part of your introduction to the vast, and frankly fascinating, world of affiliate marketing. So much so, I thought it would be worth taking a leisurely stroll down memory lane to revisit the key concepts we've encountered. After all, a good recap can really help cement those newfound understandings.

Remember how we started with the very basics? Affiliate marketing may have seemed like a bewildering forest of new concepts and processes. We spoke about the roles of merchants, affiliates, and customers, and how they each form a vital piece of the affiliate marketing puzzle. Merchants provide the products or services, affiliates promote them, and customers, well, they bring in the money. The glue that holds this all together is affiliate links and cookies, tracking sales and attributing them to the right affiliates.

But before you could jump right in, we needed to make sure your direction was clear. Setting SMART goals - those that are Specific, Measurable, Achievable, Relevant, and Time-bound - was a key element of our journey. We also delved into the world of niches, helping you to understand that identifying your specific niche, that sweet spot of passion and marketability, is key to standing out in the crowd.

Then came the first big step in setting up shop – building your online presence. Ah, remember the thrill of conceptualizing your own website, the nerve-wracking but ultimately rewarding work of crafting your social media persona, and the realization of how powerful email marketing can be? And let's not forget the basics of SEO and SEM - the lifeblood of any online business, driving organic and paid traffic to your little corner of the internet.

With your online presence in place, it was time to select the right affiliate programs. We dived into factors to consider when picking the programs, discussed the importance of researching potential affiliate programs, and even looked at the application process and approval. That might have seemed daunting, but you stuck through!

From there, we delved into the heart of your new venture – creating valuable content. It's no use having the most well-designed website or the best affiliate program if the content isn't up to scratch. We discussed the importance of quality content, how to create content that sells, how to use SEO to optimize your content, and strategies for continually creating content.

Promoting your affiliate products was next on the agenda. Through social media promotion, email marketing strategies, exploring the pros, cons, and best practices of paid advertising, and leveraging collaborations and partnerships, we developed an understanding of the many ways to get your content and affiliate links in front of your audience.

Next up, we discussed the importance of analytics, using tools for tracking performance, interpreting data, and making improvements, as well as the invaluable A/B testing. With these in your toolbox, you're able to measure your performance and make data-driven decisions.

An essential, albeit less exciting, aspect we covered was navigating the legal aspects and ethical guidelines of affiliate marketing. We discussed the importance of disclosures, not just for legal reasons but also for maintaining transparency and trust with your audience.

Finally, we talked about growing your affiliate marketing business, building relationships with merchants, diversifying your affiliate portfolio, and strategies for scaling up your business. And for a dose of inspiration, we analyzed real-life case studies of successful affiliate marketers.

Look how far you've come! From a beginner with little understanding of affiliate marketing, to a budding entrepreneur armed with knowledge, strategies, and a whole lot of potential. It's been a long journey, and you should be proud of all the progress you've made. But remember, the world of affiliate marketing is ever-evolving, and learning never truly stops. Stay curious, stay driven, and most importantly, have fun along the way!

Final Tips and Advice

Now that we're at the end of this affiliate marketing journey, it's the perfect time to offer some final nuggets of wisdom. This is your journey, and while this guide serves as a map, you have the freedom to veer off and explore. In the spirit of exploration, here are some more insights that can help you navigate the landscape of affiliate marketing.

Patience is key: Don't be disheartened if you don't see immediate results. Building a successful affiliate marketing business, like anything worthwhile, takes time. You're laying the groundwork for passive income, and that doesn't happen overnight. Keep putting in the work, creating quality content, and promoting your links, and you'll see progress.

Quality over quantity: It may be tempting to sign up for as many affiliate programs as you can, thinking it will increase your chances of making sales. But remember, your audience comes to you for your unique perspective and expertise. Promote products that you genuinely believe in and that align with your niche.

Keep learning: The digital landscape is always changing. New tools, platforms, and trends emerge regularly. Make it a point to stay updated and continually educate yourself. Attend webinars, read industry news, and join online forums and communities.

Engage with your audience: Remember, affiliate marketing isn't just about promoting products; it's about building relationships. Engage with your audience regularly. Respond to their comments, ask for their opinions, and genuinely take an interest in their needs and interests. This will help you build a loyal and engaged audience.

Be authentic: With so many affiliate marketers out there, authenticity is what sets you apart. Share your experiences, your victories as well as your challenges. This builds trust with your audience, making them more likely to value your recommendations.

Keep your website clean and user-friendly: Avoid cluttering your website with too many ads or promotions. This can deter visitors and affect your site's performance. Keep your design clean and user-friendly.

Optimize for SEO: Never underestimate the power of good SEO. Regularly update your website's SEO to ensure your content reaches the right audience. This includes using keywords appropriately, creating quality backlinks, and optimizing your site's loading speed.

Don't neglect email marketing: Building an email list is one of the most powerful tools in affiliate marketing. It allows you to communicate directly with your audience, promote your content, and build strong relationships.

Test, track, and tweak: Always be testing. Use the analytic tools at your disposal to see what's working and what isn't. Don't be afraid to tweak your strategies based on your findings.

Stay ethical and legal: Always disclose your affiliate relationships and follow all rules set by your affiliate programs. This maintains transparency with your audience and keeps you on the right side of the law.

Diversify: Don't rely on a single traffic source or a single affiliate program. Diversify your strategies to ensure a steady flow of income.

Don't give up: There will be challenges and setbacks. But remember, every successful affiliate marketer started where you are now. Keep pushing, stay motivated, and you'll make it.

And finally, remember to enjoy the journey. Affiliate marketing is a fascinating world with endless opportunities. Keep your passion alive, and that energy will reflect in your work and attract your audience. The road to passive income may be a marathon, not a sprint, but it's a race worth running.

Taking the Next Steps

As you reach the end of this guide, you might be wondering what to do next. We've covered a lot of ground from understanding affiliate marketing, setting up your online presence, creating valuable content, choosing the right affiliate programs, to optimizing performance and understanding legal aspects. But let's be clear: Reading about it is just the first step. The real journey begins when you start applying what you've learned. Let's talk about the next steps to make the leap from being a passive reader to an active affiliate marketer.

1. Action Plan: The first thing you need to do is create an action plan. It's easy to feel overwhelmed with all the information you've just absorbed, but creating a step-by-step plan can help break it down into manageable chunks. Your plan should outline what you need to do, how you're going to do it, and when you're going to do it. Take one step at a time and don't rush. Rome wasn't built in a day, and your affiliate marketing empire won't be either.

2. Setting Up: If you haven't already, start setting up your online presence. This includes your website, social media profiles, and email marketing platform. Choose your niche and your domain name carefully as these will be the pillars of your brand identity. Set up your website in a way that's clean, user-friendly, and represents you and your brand.

3. Joining Affiliate Programs: Start researching affiliate programs that align with your niche and join the ones that feel like a good fit. Remember the criteria we discussed in Chapter 5. It's not just about the commission rates; consider the product's relevance to your niche, the program's reputation, the support they offer affiliates, and other factors.

4. Creating Content: Content is king in affiliate marketing. Start brainstorming content ideas that provide value to your audience and subtly promote your affiliate products. Use the tips and strategies we discussed in Chapter 6 to create content that sells.

5. Promoting Your Content: Once you've created your content, the next step is to get it in front of your audience. Share it on your social media platforms, send it to your email list, and use SEO strategies to make it visible on search engines.

6. Tracking and Optimizing: Start tracking your performance using analytics tools. Keep an eye on your metrics to understand what's working and what's not. Use this information to optimize your strategies and improve your performance.

7. Learning and Adapting: The digital landscape is always evolving, and what works today may not work tomorrow. Always be open to learning, adapting, and evolving. Stay updated with industry news and trends, and don't be afraid to try new strategies and tools.

8. Networking: Connect with other affiliate marketers and industry professionals. Join online communities, attend events and webinars, and reach out to people you admire. Networking can open doors to collaborations, partnerships, and learning opportunities.

9. Scaling Your Business: Once you've started to see some success, it's time to think about scaling your business. Look into other traffic sources, other affiliate programs, or even creating your own product.

10. Celebrate Your Wins: Last but not least, celebrate your wins, no matter how small. Every sale, every new subscriber, every positive comment is a step in the right direction. Celebrating these wins will keep you motivated and excited about your affiliate marketing journey.

And there you have it. The next steps on your journey to becoming an affiliate marketing hero. Remember, the key is to take action. You've got the knowledge, and now it's time to apply it. It might seem scary, but every successful affiliate marketer was once in your shoes. You're ready for this. So take a deep breath, take the leap, and let's get started.

www.ingramcontent.com/pod-product-compliance
Lightning Source LLC
Chambersburg PA
CBHW070645220526
45466CB00001B/305